for the love of
Lesley

With thanks to Christopher Beddows
for his invaluable assistance

for the love of Lesley

the 'Moors Murders' remembered by a victim's mother

Ann West

Foreword by
JOHN STALKER

WARNER BOOKS

A *Warner* Book

First published in the United Kingdom
in 1989 by W H Allen

This edition published by Warner in 1993

A CIP catalogue record for this book is available
from the British Library.

ISBN 0 7515 0368 1

Photoset in North Wales by
Derek Doyle & Associates, Mold, Clwyd.
Printed and bound in Great Britain by
Clays Ltd, St Ives plc

Warner
A division of
Little, Brown and Company (UK) Limited
165 Great Dover Street
London SE1 4YA

To my beloved husband Alan,
without whom I wouldn't be here

Illustrations

Lesley Ann Downey, December 1964

Lesley with two of her brothers, Tommy and Brett, 1964

Ann with Lesley, June 1964

Myra Hindley, 1966 *(Topham Picture Library)*

Ian Brady, 1966 *(Topham Picture Library)*

Lesley's funeral, October 1965 *(Manchester Evening News)*

The funeral cortege *(Daily Express)*

Lesley's gravestone

Ann and Alan West outside Hindley's prison, 1987 *(Evening Post)*

Ian Brady *(Topham Picture Library)*

Doris Stokes, the spiritualist, 1986 *(Topham Picture Library)*

Ann West with Lord Longford, 1968 *(Manchester Evening News)*

Ann West with John Stalker *(Daily Mirror)*

Petition poster for the Murder Victims' Association

Foreword

On a cold and wet morning, three days after Christmas Day in 1964, I became part of a story which is not yet ended. Indeed I doubt that we shall ever know the full truth of it. I was at that time a 25-year-old detective sergeant in the Manchester City Police and was called in, with about a dozen other detectives, to help look for a young girl who had not returned home. That child was Lesley Ann Downey.

Over the New year holiday and for many weeks we knocked on the doors of row after row of terraced houses in the long streets off Hulme Hall Lane in Miles Platting, Manchester and of the more modern council maisonettes in Bradford Road. There was never any information of substance, but we followed up hundreds of vague sightings of her and we attempted the impossible task of tracing and interviewing every person who had attended the Boxing Day travelling fairground where she had last been seen. She seemed to have disappeared without a trace and we could not find her. The truth is that she was probably dead, many miles from her home, by the time my telephone rang calling me out to the investigation. Eventually, all of us involved in those early days of the search for her experienced the empty chill of foreboding that murder squad policemen recognise.

By the spring of 1965 most of my colleagues had gone back to their other work and I stayed on, in a part-time capacity, keeping an eye on an investigation that had run into the sand. If Lesley Ann Downey were ever to be found, something else had to happen.

It did: in October 1965 Ian Brady and Myra Hindley were arrested for the savage murder of the teenager Edward Evans and we caught our first glimpses of other murders. We know the names of those child victims now, of course: Pauline Reade, John Kilbride, Keith Bennett and Lesley Ann Downey.

As the story unfurled of what Brady and Hindley had done I remember my pain turning to horror and then to disbelief. From that day I had to readjust my understanding of the human capacity for evil. Nothing in criminal behaviour, before or since, has penetrated my heart with quite the same paralysing intensity as those emerging details of the Moors Murders. There were some tough and distinguished policemen involved in those long and distressing enquiries – Joe Mounsey, Arthur Benfield, Bob Talbot, Geoff Rimmer, Charles Abraham – but when we learned how little Lesley Ann

Downey had died, I know that part of us died as well.

I have known Lesley's mother, Ann West, since her child went missing. She is not a woman who can pretend. Her love for the memory of Lesley Ann has never diminished. But neither has the implacable hatred for the people who killed her daughter ever blazed more fiercely than it does now. She will not, she cannot, find in her heart forgiveness or understanding for what Brady and Hindley did to her child. If it is any consolation to her I can say that those feelings are shared by every policeman who worked on the case during those cold months of long ago.

But unlike her, we can remember it, sadly, and then we can put those memories away. That privilege has never been granted to Mrs West and it is probably too late now.

Even as I write, the clinging legacy of the Moors Murders shows no signs of going away. Indeed, how can it whilst the body of at least one other child still lies undiscovered beneath the dank soil of Saddleworth Moor? Ann West's life, since the death of Lesley Ann, has been rent apart by bitter and corrosive reminders of the acts of Brady and Hindley. This book is her way of making sure the rest of us do not easily forget the awful nature of those acts. I would like to hope that the writing of it will help her to find some peace in the years left to her. But I doubt that will happen. For her, peace would mean moving towards forgiveness, and her abiding love for Lesley Ann is too strong for that.

JOHN STALKER
Manchester

for the love of
Lesley

1

Last night I dreamed of Lesley. I saw her quite clearly. I saw Lesley as she was . . . timid, smiling, vulnerable. I saw Lesley as I later found her . . . broken, violated . . . dead. I lay sweating in the shadowy bedroom as the cold dawn light tried to finger its way through the curtains. I savoured the kindly pictures of my daughter that the dreams had offered. I cringed at the scenes of horror that experience told me did not begin to reach the depths of reality.

I saw Lesley with her elder brother, Terry. He was gently teasing her as he did in life. She was laughing uncertainly and turning those exquisite blue eyes up to him for confirmation of some doubt. I saw Lesley's body being buried in the secrecy of night on the cold and terrible moor. I watched another picture of Lesley . . .

her eyes wide open in unbelieving death as the wet peat was scraped over her to hide a foul secret from the world.

I clenched my fingers tightly together to stop the scream that was aching in my throat. There was no reason why Alan should be awoken. He had suffered enough with me. I tried to cleanse my mind with memories of Lesley at better times . . . times when she was free and alive and happy. I saw her gliding proudly round the play area below the flat. She was proud of her roller skates and I was proud of the skill she showed in her unconscious grace. I almost laughed as I suddenly recalled something that had been forgotten for years. I had looked over the balcony one day and seen Lesley pulling her little brother Brett at some speed. She had somehow secured his feet into the skates and with a belt as a tow rope was giving him a wonderful, if highly dangerous ride. Suddenly I remembered the tears that had sprung to her eyes as Alan told her off for being irresponsible. You never had to raise a finger to Lesley. She understood immediately when she had done something silly.

How could she have understood the nightmare that she suffered at the hands of her sadistic killers? I heard the scream again last night – the same scream I heard on the terrible tape in that office at the police station so many years ago. I heard Lesley crying out for me – the cry became a scream and I couldn't shut it out or make it stop.

With the strange logic of dreams I suddenly found

2

myself in church. There was beautiful singing from the choir and I looked and saw the space that had been left where Lesley used to sing. Suddenly the singing became harsh and discordant. They were not singing; they were raising their voices in a shrill and rising scream that filled the church until my head was aching with the sound.

The scream died in my head, to be replaced by fairground music, confused and clashing sounds and rhythms swirling round the crowded images of my dream. I was desperately searching for my daughter, aware that if I found her she would be safe but if I failed then something more horrible than imagining was waiting for her. I was fighting against the crowds that were a solid barrier in my way. I thought I caught glimpses of her in the distance but she was being led away. I shouted but no sound would come from my throat. The music blared harshly and arms were pulling me back. I wanted to shout 'Don't trust them Lesley! Don't listen to them!' But she was gone.

The kaleidoscope of sound and wildly whirling images settled into a silent landscape of the night. A pale, cold wash of moonlight lit the scene and I realised I knew that place where my dream had taken me. I was walking down straight and rigid paths with grave stones towering all around me. Angels in Victorian marble and great granite crosses shone in the sickly light. I was desperately reading the lettering on the headstones. I was searching for a name. Names and dates and verses swam before my eyes but still the name for which I searched evaded me. I started to run and the ground

3

moved effortlessly beneath my feet. Then I knew where I was going. I didn't need to look for names anymore. I knew where I was going but it was important that I get there as soon as possible. I ran as if I had no weight. I floated over the ground. I could see the grave I sought. There was somebody there already. I tried to call out but the small figure could not hear me. I knew who it was and my heart beat wildly. Although I was moving like the wind I could get no closer. The figure was moving away.

'Lesley! Wait for me . . . Lesley!'

But the scream was silent and the figure faded. I reached out desperately but I was too late. I lay on the cold grass in tearful exhaustion. The headstone that I know so well stood above me in the deepening darkness. I didn't need the fading moonlight to see what was written there. In the drowning depths of my dream I reached out a cold finger and traced the letters chiselled into the stone and into my heart –

Lesley Ann Downey . . . A little flower lent not given . . . to bud on earth and bloom in heaven

I slept terribly last night. I should be used to it now. That dream has haunted me day and night for 25 years.

2

How and where do I begin? How do I tell the story of a life that for the last quarter of a century has been totally dominated by a senseless and sadistic act of murder? Why, after all these years, am I still haunted by the brutal madness that took my little girl away from me? Each day I think of Lesley, pray to her and try to rid myself of the images that haunt me – images that have haunted many mothers and fathers since the graves on that terrible moor started to reveal their secrets.

Twenty-five years may seem a long time ago. It may seem like history to some. For many it will be a blur of half-remembered names, fashions and fads, popular songs, political scandals . . . But for me 25 years ago is yesterday. It is Lesley giving me a hug and promising not to be late back from the fair, Lesley sitting with me to examine her Christmas presents. It is all so close I could reach out and touch it.

Those other names now so closely linked with Lesley's meant nothing to anyone at the time. Hundreds of children go missing every year. Some return. Some are found. Some disappear, forever. Now we know, or in some cases suspect, what happened to these particular children. The files are still open. The legacy of those grim days 25 years ago is as follows:

> **Pauline Reade,** aged sixteen, from Gorton, Manchester: disappeared July 1963;
> **John Kilbride,** aged twelve, from Ashton, Manchester: disappeared November 1963;
> **Keith Bennett,** aged twelve, from Longsight, Manchester: disappeared June 1964;
> **Lesley Ann Downey,** aged ten, from Miles Platting, Manchester: disappeared December 1964;
> **Edward Evans,** aged seventeen, from Ardwick, Manchester: axed to death October 1965.

The above, and probably others as well, were selected by Ian Brady and Myra Hindley for a calculated ritual of cold-blooded torture and sexual humiliation, followed by their murder. With the exception of that of Edward Evans the children's bodies were taken onto Saddleworth Moor and buried in shallow, unmarked graves.

Little in the background of Brady, who was born in Glasgow in 1938, or Hindley, who was born in Manchester in 1942, offers any clue to their grotesque behaviour. Can anything explain why they should have put those children through such physical and emotional agonies? I have come to believe, together with others who have knowledge of their depraved practices, that both are evil. They carry around with them a ruthless force that drives them to terrorise and slaughter. The force is still within them. It will die only when they die.

Brady and Hindley were discovered in October 1965 when the hacked corpse of Edward Evans was found, wrapped in a carpet, upstairs in the house they were occupying in Hattersley. The police had been tipped off by Hindley's brother-in-law Dave Smith, who panicked at his growing involvement with the murdering couple. They had not had time to bury Evans on the moor with all their other 'sacrificial' victims. Later, tape-recordings and photographs would reveal some of the grave sites on the moors. Brady was in the habit of recording them for posterity, with Hindley posing on the graves. In the case of my Lesley the tapes and photographs recorded something unutterably worse: the slow, deliberate torture and sexual humiliation of a little child prior to her casual murder.

Soon after the murder Brady was charged, and so, a few days later, was Hindley. Despite a very strong suspicion on the part of the police that many more children were buried on the moors or otherwise disposed of by Brady and Hindley it was with the murders of John Kilbride, Edward Evans and Lesley Ann Downey that the pair were charged. For three weeks at Chester Assizes in April and May of 1966 they tried to maintain that they were not guilty, but finally Brady was convicted of all three murders; Hindley was found guilty of two, and also of being an accessory after the fact in the case of John Kilbride. Both were sentenced to life imprisonment after a trial at which revelations were made that horrified the whole nation.

They may be merely the tip of an iceberg. Pauline Reade's body has since been found. Keith Bennett's is still lost on the moor. How many more might there be? Some have calculated that another nine victims may have been randomly selected by Brady for slaughter. How many did Hindley know about or assist in? In the late 1970s the possibility of parole arose for Myra Hindley, although Ian Brady has consistently said that he does not wish to be considered for it. Hindley's case was championed by Lord Longford, who found himself with some very strange supporters, some of them from the underworld of vice and prostitution, in his crazy campaign to release this child-killer on to the streets.

The national press together with organised public protest combined to ensure that Longford failed in that particular attempt. But unfounded rumours of Hindley's transformation into a model prisoner continue to be printed in the press and to infiltrate the public's consciousness. Lord Longford and similarly confused 'do-gooders' still seek to obtain Hindley's release on parole.

Would they continue their efforts if they had heard and seen what I have? I heard Hindley torturing my 10-year-old daughter. I heard Lesley's screams as she begged for mercy. I saw her body after Hindley and Brady had hidden the evidence of their monstrous

8

appetites on the moor. If remorse is known to Myra Hindley, may she live long to feel its pain. But in my darkest moments my hope is not just that she should suffer in life but that she should endure a long death, that she should die slowly . . . as slowly as my daughter and the others they took so cruelly from this world.

It may be thought from such remarks that I have strayed into emotional, vengeance-filled fantasies. As far as I am concerned I am convinced that if that sadistic pervert Myra Hindley is ever released from gaol I will ensure that she does not enjoy her freedom for long. The power of love is very strong, but so is the power of hate. Both have kept me going over the years. My health and happiness have been destroyed by my frustrated love for Lesley Ann and my loathing for her bestial killers, but I have survived. This book is about survival. It is about those who have helped me with their unselfish love. It is about and for the love of Lesley.

3

Morning, Boxing Day 1964. The kids were still in their rooms playing with the presents that had survived Christmas Day and I was tidying the sitting room while waiting for the kettle to boil in the kitchen. I could hear Alan singing to himself in the bathroom. I felt good. The previous day had been a success. It had been the best Christmas Day for years. I listened to the laughter of the kids upstairs and thought how lucky we were. It had not always been like this.

I looked out of the window and saw the decorations in the rooms of the flats on the other side of the street. This year, thanks to Alan's contribution to the family finances, *we* had a tree. After my divorce from Terry Downey two years previously things seemed to be settling down at last. The council had housed us after moves too numerous to mention and the future seemed set fair.

I shivered, but it was not with cold. I had suddenly remembered where the children and I had been less than a year ago. After all the scenes with Terry about his womanising and stingy treatment of the children I had taken Lesley and the boys and left. I had been used to being fairly self-sufficient; my own mother had died when I was ten at the beginning of the war and Dad, who was a regimental sergeant-major, had let my grandfather bring me up. Even occasional contact with my father ceased when he was taken prisoner in Germany during the war. I had learned fairly quickly to fend for myself.

But the year prior to this one had stretched even my patience.

It was 1963 and so desperate was I to find a home for the children that I had squatted for several months in an empty private house. This was before squatting became common among the homeless. There was no particular precedent, just a terrible need to put a roof over the heads of my children and provide some sort of base, however insecure. The council was outraged, but I had never been one to bow down to authority and when they protested and tried to get us out I pointed out that all they had to do was provide us with some council accommodation and all would be well. They didn't like my tactics. However, we moved into a council flat in Charnley Walk in the spring of 1964.

I heard Alan call from the kitchen, asking if I wanted a

coffee. Alan had made it all perfect. Now I had a place for my family and a kind, generous man whom the children were already beginning to look on as a father.

'Here you are, love,' said Alan in his broad Cockeny accent, which still made me smile. The coffee was welcome and we sat on the sofa and stretched out our legs, ready for the day ahead. It was good to be with Alan although it was strange to have him to myself as he was normally on the road with the furniture delivery van at all sorts of hours or romping with his ready-made family.

'What are you thinking, love?'

I laughed. I was thinking, as it happened, of the chaotic courtship that had transformed our lives during the last few months. Life had never been dull since that chance meeting with Alan in the St Vincent's pub on Oldham Road earlier in the year. It was I who hadn't wanted any involvement with a man at that time. The pain of a failed marriage and the relief of having found a house at last made the complications of a new relationship something I wished to avoid.

'I was remembering when we met, love,' I replied.

'It was a bit of a lark, wasn't it?' he laughed, giving my hand a friendly squeeze.

It had certainly been a lark – a crazy fling in which, despite myself, I found myself thinking more and more of Alan when he was back in London. The time until he had a delivery to make in the north dragged by too slowly and I found myself, over the weeks, looking forward to his arrival more and more. His deliveries and the van came to mean a lot in my life. It was the furniture van that became our rather cumbersome 'taxi' round Manchester.

On that first night we met I had been having a quiet drink with the girls – it was a sort of hen party, I suppose. I noticed Alan with a couple of other fellows. My attention was drawn to him when one of his mates called out to him at the bar and called him 'Twink'. I smiled to myself as I realised the reason for the nickname. He had very attractive, naturally curly black hair and there was a perming agent of that name on the market at the time. I didn't want any involvement; I had come out for a night with the girls, but my friend Betty was all for having some fun. Before I knew what was happening it was closing time and we were all bundling into Alan's huge furniture delivery van and heading through the streets to the Mancunian Club. It wasn't the most sophisticated form of transport but it was a laugh.

That had been the beginning. Now, a couple of years later, Alan was here, looking at the Christmas cards on the window-sill. The scene was domestic, comfortable . . . In just a few months we had settled into the sort of family life that I had never really experienced before. It had taken a long time but at last the children and I had found peace and contentment. Alan had made it all complete.

Life was never dull with Alan. There was always something to look forward to. Sometimes he let his sense of humour run away with him. The day of the telegram was a typical example. It was about a week after I had

13

met Alan and we had gone 'clubbing' in the delivery van. Lesley came running into the kitchen with a telegram that had just been delivered.

'Open it, Mum. It must be important.' Her eyes were large and stared at me in concern. She always took life seriously, although she was never moody. I hastily ripped open the brown envelope and read it aloud.

'UP TONIGHT. SEE YOU . . . TWINK'.

Lesley looked at me in astonishment and for a moment it meant little to me. Suddenly I realised . . . Twink – of course! Alan later explained that he had stopped at Leek in Staffordshire and impulsively decided that he wanted to see me again. The telegram was the result. Lesley and the boys teased me unmercifully when I explained that I was going to meet Twink that night.

I nearly didn't meet Alan that night, as it turned out. I waited for an hour at the St Vincent's pub, but no Alan. I was making a bitter lemon last another five minutes when he breezed in with a casual apology. He had arrived early, parked the wagon round the corner and fallen asleep. If he hadn't woken up in time I don't think we would have had a future together! As it turned out we had a fun evening in town but when he drove me home later that night in the largest 'taxi' in Greater Manchester there began a long-running lie that must have been increasingly frustrating to Alan. He asked if he could come in for a coffee to keep him awake on the long journey back to base in London. I refused, claiming that my mother who lived with us would be disturbed.

Visit after visit Alan was waved goodbye from the

doorstep as 'Mother' kept him at arm's length. I think he even drove away slowly so as not to disturb the old lady. Of course, the cat was let out of the bag eventually – but not by me. I was beginning to find the presence of the fictitious old lady a bit of a nuisance myself but I didn't know how to get rid of her. One evening the van was parked at the end of Charnley Walk after an evening out with Alan. I popped inside to see if the kids were all right, leaving Alan with my friend Betty who was due to be dropped off at her house later. In my absence Betty 'grassed' on me and explained the situation to Alan. I'm not sure if Alan got his cup of coffee for the road that night but it was not long before he moved in with us. It was unconventional at the time but we loved each other and the children had taken to him so what was the harm?

The children couldn't help but be captivated by his cheeky sense of humour and his madcap pranks. Our unofficial holiday in Kirkcaldy was typical. With hardly an hour's notice Alan had called with a van full of sofa-beds and announced that we were going to Scotland. To me it was mad, but to the kids it was a real-life adventure. After all, not every child can claim to have spent the night on a sofa-bed in the back of a delivery wagon in Scotland. We could vouch for the sofas' comfort, too.

'Do you remember Kirkcaldy, Alan?' I asked him.

He turned from the window and there was a twinkle in his eye. 'Not half, doll!' I remember thinking that his nickname was well deserved . . . and not just because of his curly hair.

The kids were starting to get noisy upstairs. We smiled at each other. It was good, our being together. It was a good christmas and it wasn't over yet. Nostalgia was all very well but it was the turn of the year and so much lay ahead. I busied myself making a late breakfast for Alan and the children. Life had meaning and purpose again.

4

Afternoon, Boxing Day 1964. I eased myself into the chair by the electric fire and promised myself half an hour before making the tea. It had been a real family Christmas with Alan and the kids. The Christmas dinner had been well appreciated, the presents pronounced more than satisfactory by Terry, Tommy and Brett, and Lesley had been over the moon about Santa's gifts.

'I want to be Bobby's girl . . . Bobby's girl . . .'

From upstairs Lesley Ann was singing her song – the song that had dominated the pop charts and our maisonette for the whole of the holiday. Perhaps Susan Maugham's picture would soon be joining the poster of Chris Montez.

'Come on, Les, *White Christmas* is on the telly in a couple of minutes!' Alan shouted.

'Not *again*,' groaned Tommy, releasing his well-sucked thumb for a moment. Tommy was still tired from a sleepless night on Christmas Eve after the excitement of helping Alan decorate the tree. '*White Christmas* is sloppy. Even Brett would sleep through that.' But Brett was already asleep dreaming whatever innocent dreams 4-year-olds have.

'Mum, will you help me with my sewing?' Lesley called downstairs.

'Of course, love. We can do it in front of the television.'

'Thanks, you're a love.'

A sound of rapid feet on the stairs and she was next to me, wriggling deep into the chair at my side.

'Are you sure Terry can't go to the fair with us? He could wrap up.'

I paused in threading the needle and glanced through the window. It had been a bright, dry day but there was a look of more snow in the air.

'I don't think so, doll. It'll be slushy underfoot. Mrs Clark's going, isn't she? Our Terence is best staying where he is.'

'Pity. Perhaps you can come with me tomorrow, Terry.'

'Hey, we're not made of money, Les,' said Alan. 'You can have a tanner and that's it. The Gas Board pays about as much as Scrooge – in case you hadn't noticed.'

We laughed and the decision seemed to have been made . . . or made itself. Lesley Ann and Tommy would go to the fair on the recreation ground for an hour before tea with Mrs Clark from downstairs and their daughter Linda. Silcock's Wonder Fair was a well-run show with some good rides. It came every Christmas on its tour. We'd all have tea afterwards and perhaps . . .

'Terry, do you feel like going through that new tune of Lesley's with her after tea? What is it, love?'

' "Save the Last Dance for Me" . . . the Drifters.'

'I haven't got the chords. Besides, we're not exactly London Palladium standard.'

'You've got to be older than fourteen to play on the stage,' chipped in Tommy.

'You'll be lucky to survive eight if we have any more cheek from you,' grunted Terry in between sniffles.

'I wish we still had that tape of you two performing . . . now, *what* was that song?'

"Bobby's Girl",' they all cried out mockingly. Lesley blushed with pleasure and embarrassment. She was beginning to come out of herself but was still a shy, quiet girl.

'There, that's got you started. Try to keep the stitches small. I've got to put some mince pies on or else we'll be short at tea.'

'Not more mince pies!' moaned Terry and gave a wink at Lesley as I left for the kitchen.

The serving hatch between the kitchen and the sitting room was half open and as I rolled pastry and cut out tops and bottoms I glanced in at the family occasionally. All in their different ways were enjoying themselves and in my way so was I. The kitchen was hot with the oven on and I opened the window. The sound of the music from the different rides at the fair was suddenly competing with Bing Crosby from the television. The early evening sky above the recreation ground was already showing the garish lights of the stalls and rides. There was a sudden rush of cold air – at least, something caused me to shiver – and I shut the window.

Suddenly Brett was behind me hugging my legs.

'Can you make some mince pies for Rebel?'

I pulled the hatch shut quietly. I didn't want Lesley upset at talk of Rebel. We'd had enough arguments with the council about keeping a cocker spaniel in the flat and Lesley was still upset when she thought of 'her dog' having to live with an uncle.

'I think Rebel will be full of turkey, Brett,' I said quietly and gave him a kiss. He nodded his 4-year-old head wisely and shuffled back to the family. I put the mince pies in the oven and thanked God for such a good-natured family. I included Alan in these thoughts. In the couple of years we had been together even the children had begun to think of him as their father. We had a lot to be thankful for.

I went back and sat with Lesley again.

'How's the sewing coming along then, love?' I asked, ruffling her short, curly hair. I still couldn't get used to it being cut short. For ten years it had grown steadily till it reached right down her back. Still, it pleased her to have it cut in the new fashion and she did look bonny.

'Not bad, but I'm not going to win any prizes for needlework,' Lesley giggled, giving my arm a quick squeeze.

Tommy suddenly jumped up from the floor at our feet.

'Can we be going now?' he demanded. 'We're not going to have much time if you want us back for teatime.'

Lesley put her sewing kit on the arm of the chair and sat forward.

'Can we, Mum? Is it OK, Dad?'

Alan smiled. It was good that the kids were calling him 'Dad' quite naturally. He could never deny Lesley anything – at least when he could afford it.

'Wrap up warm, miss. We don't want two of you down with 'flu.'

'Are you sure you can't come, Terry?' she asked him with her little smile.

'He can't come,' said Alan quietly. 'Mrs Clark will see you don't get up to any pranks.'

'Can I put my new trews on? It'll be cold out there on the Red Rec.'

'Of course you can, love – and put your blue coat on.'

The sound of her light footsteps on the stairs faded.

I watched the last of the film before checking the oven. It was a quarter to four and the lights of the fair lit the darkening sky like a weird sunset. Terry had fallen asleep but Tommy was by the front door putting on his parka, obviously anxious to get his pennies spent on the rides and sideshows

'Come on, Les!' he shouted.

'A minute ... just a minute,' she called from her bedroom.

'When you've spent your money we want you both back here sharpish,' said Alan. 'Your mum's laying tea for five o'clock and you'll need to get cleaned up after the fair.'

Suddenly Lesley came down the stairs. In her blue coat and trews with little blue shoes she looked a picture.

' 'Bout time,' grumbled Tommy.

'Come here, doll-face, and give us a kiss for Christmas,' laughed Alan, feeling as proud as I did at Lesley's appearance.

We all exchanged hugs and kisses and then they were gone. Alan turned the television down and asked me if I was going back into the kitchen. I said I was.

'Come on. I've got an idea.'

'What are you up to?' I demanded as he opened the front door on to the cold balcony. He bustled me out into the chill.

'Here, make snowballs,' he laughed, scraping a layer of last night's snow from the guard rail.

'Are you daft?' I said. 'We're a bit old for snowball fights.'

'For the kids when they get back,' he explained. 'We can bomb them, as they come across the play area.'

The gas-holder at the end of Charnley Walk towered into the evening sky. I craned over the balcony to see whether the kids were still in sight. They had disappeared. Like kids ourselves Alan and I scraped a little pile of snowballs together for when Tommy and Lesley Ann returned. There was a smell of snow in the air. The music from the fairground sounded tinny and cheap. I shivered suddenly.

'Alan, let's go in. I've tea to prepare.'

So we went in and tidied the sitting room and enjoyed the last hour of unspoilt happiness in our lives. It was just past four o'clock.

5

Early evening, Boxing Day 1964. The front door opened. We turned expectantly. Tommy rushed in, his cheeks rosy and eyes bright from the cold.

'Where's Lesley?' I asked.

He looked puzzled for a second.

'I thought she was back ahead of me. Isn't she here, then?'

Alan looked annoyed. I felt mildly disturbed.

'Didn't you see her there? I thought you met up at the fair.'

'It was very busy. I saw her, though. She was on the wall of death last time I got a glimpse.'

I looked at Alan. His concern was infectious. Tommy stood looking rather nervously from one to the other of us.

'Go and see if she's with Mrs Clark downstairs,' I suggested. 'They probably came back ahead of you.'

Tommy dashed off, slamming the door behind him. I could hear his feet on the concrete stairway.

'Elsie will be here soon. I'd best be getting the kettle on.'

Alan nodded and turned to the television with a slight frown on his face. I busied myself making final preparations for tea. Lesley would be back any minute. She doted on her Aunty Elsie and wouldn't be late for her for the world. I could hear the jolly music from the television in the sitting room. It would be all right.

But it wasn't all right. Twenty minutes passed and I was about to go down to Mrs Clark's myself when Tommy burst through the door again. He was breathless and white in the face. Alan came into the kitchen, Tommy breathlessly blurted out his story.

'I've been to Mrs Clark's but she didn't go. I've been down to the Rec again but she's nowhere to be seen . . .'

'Hold on a minute,' said Alan. 'Who didn't go?'

'Mrs Clark didn't go to the fair. She was tired and didn't feel like going. Their Linda went with Lesley. I've just been over to the fair again but I can't see her. I've looked everywhere – honest.'

Terry appeared in the door of the kitchen. He was white-faced and feverish. There was a frightened look on his face.

'Get back in front of the fire, love,' I said distractedly. I could feel the turmoil rise physically in my chest. I was looking wildly through the kitchen window at the garish lights of the fair lighting up the sky above the flats. Alan's hand was on my shoulder. He tried to calm the panic that was beginning to infect all of us.

'Do as your mother says, Terry. Tommy, you've done your best. I think we'd better see if Lesley's with any of her schoolmates.'

I nodded dumbly. Although it was still only half-past five something was beginning to gnaw at me from within. I was at the door before Alan stopped me.

'It's cold. Here.'

He put a coat into my hands and waited while I struggled into it. My hands wouldn't work and he patiently buttoned me up before opening the door and leading me out into the winter dark. The windows of the street showed warm lights, Christmas trees and decorations strung from curtain rails and chimney breasts. It felt very cold out in the empty darkness. I was aware for a moment of the tinny sound of fairground music. I shivered involuntarily and we set about our task.

Lesley's schoolfriends all lived within a short distance of the flat so it did not take too long to cover the likely houses. Every door we knocked on was a door of hope. Each time a door was answered I waited for Lesley's apologetic face to appear, explaining how she had forgotten the time. Instead, the concerned apologies of parents and friends drove my forlorn hope deeper and deeper into the emptiness of growing despair. I looked at Alan's face, pale and ill-looking in the sodium glare of the street lights.

'The Red Rec – come on. Tommy could have missed her. He said it was swarming with people.'

I nodded and we dashed, hand in hand, through the empty streets and lanes that led down to the fair. There was noise and confusion and people pressing towards the shooting galleries, rides, stalls and hot-dog stands. There was the smell of onions. People's breath rose in the chill December air. The insistent din of the music changed as we went from ride to ride and stall to stall. There was no sign of Lesley.

Breathless queries and descriptions of Lesley to busy men and boys in charge of taking pennies from the happy, noisy crowd were met with casual shakes of the head or curt denials of knowledge. We were just another panicky couple worrying needlessly about a child who had spent too long at the fair. We were nothing unusual. To them Lesley was just another kid who was going to get a telling-off when she turned up late for tea.

I stood in bewilderment as the Ferris wheel and the crowd's cries of delight whirled up and around me.

'Come on, love – she's not here.'

Alan was taking my arm and leading me away from the confusion and disappointment of the place. We hurried through the cold streets, each of us hoping against hope that she would be waiting, shamefaced, at home.

Terry's face said it all: his look of expectation as we rushed in changed in an instant to frightened concern on seeing we were alone. There were no words. Alan and I dashed downstairs to Mrs Clark as Terry ran upstairs to the bedroom.

All my fear and confusion burst out in hysterical accusations and angry threats when we got to the Clarks'. I raved at Mary for not going to the wretched fair. Almost out of control, I accused them of negligence, cursed them for being so irresponsible as to allow a 9-year-old like Linda to go on her own with Lesley. Her guilt and my fury were a potent and explosive mixture. The air rang with our shouting.

Finally Alan and Roy Clark intervened. I can't remember what was said, but finally there was silence . . . silence, not calm. Adrenalin was pumping through my bloodstream. I had to be moving constantly. I had to do something. Lesley was out there somewhere. My daughter was waiting for me to come and take her home.

We were in the street again. Alan and Roy were talking to a group of about a dozen neighbours and friends. Terry was holding on to my arm. I wasn't sure who was supporting whom. It was no use trying to make him stay inside. I could sense the guilt he felt. Why hadn't he gone with Lesley? Why had he stayed in and given in to his 'flu? I hugged him to try to tell him that we didn't blame him . . . that he shouldn't blame himself. He shook his head. He was a confused 14-year-old who was about to be catapulted into a cruel and premature adulthood.

To the fair again . . . down the cold and lonely streets again. More questions and the same agonising, negative replies. People split up in pairs and searched and questioned along the thronged alleys between the stalls and rides. Twice I gasped with momentary relief as a blue coat amongst the crowds sent me barging, hysterical and careless, to catch Lesley in my arms. Twice I stopped at the last second as a face that was not Lesley's turned with puzzled curiosity to see what I wanted and I called out desperatley and pushed towards her. I was dimly aware of people nudging each other and pointing me out with disapproving looks on their faces. The same questions . . . the same answers.

Alan was at my shoulder. Above the screams from the wall of death I could hear him urgently trying to tell me something. He was leading me away to the edge of the Rec.

'You go home, love. There's some of us going to check along the bank of the stream.'

My stomach turned over. This was something else. This was something I had not even contemplated. Lesley was lost . . . or with some friends . . . or with somebody that she'd met . . . nothing worse than that. I shook my head violently.

'There's no need. She's all right. She's *with* somebody, that's all.'

He nodded. 'We've got to check, though, Ann. Go on home.' I clung to his arm. If he was going with the others to check the stream I must go as well. I was her mother, wasn't I? No mother sits at home waiting when her daughter is missing.

I was to learn in all the months that followed just how much waiting at home a mother does, how much waiting and telling lies to herself.

As we walked the slushy banks of the stream all I

29

could see was the odd reflection of garish light from the fair at our backs. The sounds of amplified music swelled above the shouts and laughter. A chill ran down my back as I suddenly picked out the tune that was filtering its way through the confusing racket . . . 'Let's Dance' . . . Chris Montez . . . an insistent, jingling rhythm. Another of Lesley's favourite songs! It was an omen, but whether for good or ill I didn't know. We left the stream and headed for Charnley Walk, making a last search of the fair as we returned.

'She'll be OK, Ann.'

'Don't worry. She'll be back.'

'Sorry, Alan. I'm sure it'll be all right.'

'Get a drink down you. It's brass monkey weather!'

And our little search party dispersed. We looked up at the flat. Neither of us wanted to move. We were delaying the moment that would bring either joyous relief or despair.

'Come on!'

Terry flung open the door and rushed through the flat calling his sister's name in every room. There was no reply. We stood in the hall and looked at each other in blank, hollow desperation. The night was just beginning.

In a matter of minutes we got the kids sitting down in front of the television and a neighbour coming in to look after them, then Alan and I took another walk through the streets, this time to report Lesley's disappearance to the police.

'Mill Street . . . that's the nearest one, isn't it?' Alan asked as we trotted to the end of Charnley Walk.

'I think so,' I mumbled, the fact of bringing the police into our fears seeming to nudge the whole situation on to a different and even more frightening plane.

No buses ran at that time of night towards Mill Street so we set off, walking as rapidly as possible along the length of Bradford Road with the towering gas-holders watching us . . . pathetic, worried little people in the throes of growing confusion. Hulme Hall Lane . . . quickly, Alan, quickly . . . Albert Road . . . Mill Street. Over there . . . on the left . . . quickly!

I was breathless and panic-stricken as we stumbled through the door to face a rather bored and world-weary desk sergeant.

'Can I help you?'

'Oh God,' I thought, 'I hope so.'

'Our little girl's gone missing. She went to the fair –'

The desk sergeant's eyes didn't flicker. He nodded calmly.

'How long?'

'An hour . . . an hour or so,' I stuttered. This man's matter-of-fact tone was starting to irritate me. Didn't he realise how important this was?

'Listen to me,' I shouted. 'It doesn't matter how long she's been gone. It's not like Lesley. I know her!'

The infuriating sergeant drummed his pencil on the counter-top. He smiled at Alan as if sorry for him having to cope with this silly female.

'Apart from the fact that it's Christmas and we have a number of officers on leave, there is no way we can mount a search for a kiddy that's an hour late home. If we did that every time a child gets reported missing we'd never have time to do anything else.'

'But it's my Lesley!' I screamed at him. 'My Lesley is *never* late.' I looked to Alan for support.

'It's true. Lesley has never done anything like this before. It's totally out of character,' Alan explained patiently.

'And you are the girl's father?' enquired the sergeant wearily.

'No, I'm Alan West. I live with Mrs Downey at Charnley Walk.'

I noticed the slightest raising of an eyebrow. 'Look, the best thing you can do is go right home and wait. She might well be there waiting for you by now. Ninety per cent of cases like this are false starts.'

'But she's not –'

'Please, Mrs Downey. I'm sure you'll find I'm right.'

I fumed inwardly. How did he know what my Lesley was like? If we were a 'case', then why wasn't he treating us like one?

As if reading my mind he went through the motions of writing our names and address in the logbook.

'If she's not back by . . .' he checked the station clock, 'say, eleven or eleven-thirty, then come back and we'll look into it.'

I started to rage at the matter-of-fact way we were being treated, but then Alan took me by the shoulders. I felt his strength and he whispered to me that I was not to get any more upset. In a daze of disbelief and confusion we found ourselves out on the pavement. There was a thin cover of snow and flakes were still dancing in the sickly glow from the street lamps.

'Tracker dogs,' I muttered to Alan.

'You what? What are you on about?' Alan demanded. He was nearing the end of his tether.

'This snow will make it impossible for tracker dogs to follow her. This delay is ridiculous!' My voice suddenly rose to a scream.

Alan stopped me under a lamp-post as we trudged back towards Charnley Walk. He took my face in his hands and looked into my eyes very fiercely. 'Just remember that I love her too. We are going to find her. Never let go of that thought.' His expression softened. 'She maybe waiting for us now. Let's go!'

And we ran through the cold streets, allowing a little warmth into our hearts from the terrible hope that led us towards the rest of that long Saturday.

6

Late evening, Boxing Day 1964. The snowballs still lay on the balcony silently mocking us. Terry, Tommy, Brett and our neighbour Margaret Glennen turned hopeful faces to us as we stumbled through the door. No words were said at first. None were needed. I started to take my coat off but Alan stopped me.

'Wait, love . . . just a sec.'

He looked thoughtful for a moment.

'What is it?' I tugged angrily at his sleeve. 'What have you remembered?'

'I've not remembered anything, but we can't just sit around here till the police start to take us seriously, can we?'

'The fair again?'

'No . . . but there is that derelict mill.'

'What derelict mill?' I snapped. 'What would she be doing at a derelict mill?'

'What's she doing not coming back on time?' he retorted. 'We can't sit around doing nothing. These could be vital hours.'

Alan's quiet determination convinced me. Pausing only to try to settle the kids and ask Margaret if she would hang on for a little while longer, I followed Alan out into the streets again.

'Which mill, Alan?' I gasped, trying to keep up with his long, hurrying strides.

'The old cotton mill on Butler Street. Kids sometimes mess around in there.'

'But it's not like Lesley to go to a place like that. It doesn't make sense.'

'*None* of this makes sense! Come on . . .'

And I followed him, suddenly aware of the desperation that was driving him–that would not allow him to rest – that was forcing him to clutch at straws of possibility. We were both clutching at straws, but what else was there to do? Lurching like drunks across the broken bricks of the dark wasteland that surrounded the towering, gaunt skeleton of the victorian mill, we called Lesley's name repeatedly into the cold blackness. With no torch to guide us we fumbled and staggered into the dangerous dark of the mill floor.

'Lesley! Lesley!'

A pause and then the thin empty echo would come back to us; the echo of our own desperate voices . . . never the voice we ached to hear calling to us.

'Lesley!' I screamed. But there was only the empty echo. My throat was raw.

'Leave it, love. She's not here.' Alan's voice was sad and resigned. He took my arm in the blackness of that long-dead mill and led me out into the glare of the street lights and home. We didn't allow ourselves to hope this time. As we threaded our way back through Miles Platting to our own area we struggled to dismiss the fantasy of seeing Lesley waiting for us in the sitting room . . . Lesley waving to us from the balcony . . . Lesley running towards us down the wet and glistening pavements. We struggled to avoid the fantasy but it haunted us nevertheless, and like all fantasies it doomed us to disappointment.

The disappointment was not ours alone. The boys were all tearful by now. They could not understand what was going on. This was Christmas . . . this was not how Christmas was supposed to be. I took Tommy and Brett to bed after reassuring Margaret that we would definitely call on her if there was anything we needed. There was only one thing we needed and the passing hours were taking her further and further away.

'Don't worry. No one will hurt her...they couldn't!'

Despite Terry's fierce protest as he turned his face up to me from his seat by the television I had begun to fear what at that time I would have called 'the worst'. Time has taught me a new meaning to that phrase. I ruffled his hair and attempted an approximation of a smile. 'You're right, Terry. I'm sure you're right.' And as I said it I began to believe again in Lesley's safety.

I don't know for how long we sat and tried to puzzle out some solution to the mystery. We didn't have time to feel weary as our minds were in constant activity considering and rejecting possible reasons that would explain Lesley's absence. Suddenly I realised that the tea lay untouched upon the table . . . the tea that my sister Elsie and her husband John had been due to share with us.

'Alan! Elsie and John . . . they didn't come. Don't you see? Lesley could have decided to go to them – to surprise them!'

Alan looked up at me, doubt in his eyes. And then the doubt cleared as he considered the distant possibility. Another straw to clutch at. Another door opening.

Having no phone, we had to set off down the streets once more to catch a bus to Elsie's house. At one point a niggling doubt about Lesley's ability to pay the bus fare came into my mind. She'd had sixpence for the fair but that wouldn't have gone very far and she couldn't have walked the seven or so miles to her Aunty Elsie's . . . not unless she got a lift from somebody . . . a lift from a stranger . . . Oh God, why can't this bus go any faster?

We found John and Elsie with their friends Mary and John. Puzzled faces gave way to expressions of concern, and there were explanations about intending to come over later, apologies about missing tea, questions and suggestions, reassurances and concerned glances. No Lesley. Another broken straw.

We travelled back together on the bus, Elsie and John and their friends, gazing out of the windows, looking for a face in the crowds that were starting to occupy the streets heading for pubs and clubs. There was no blue coat, no curly black hair, no smiling face searching amongst the Boxing Day merry-makers for a face that she knew. I stared at my reflection in the window of the bus and saw a drawn face looking back at me, devoid of emotion and of animation. It was nearly half-past eight. Lesley was three and a half hours late home.

'You never know,' said Elsie encouragingly as we turned once more up Charnley Walk, 'she might be there waiting for us.' I shook my head in denial. No more false hope, no more disappointment . . . please. There was some talk, more guessing, more attempts at reassurance and then they were all leaving.

'Are you sure you and Alan won't come for a drink with us?'

I shook my head. It might still be Boxing Day for some, but we were separated from that world now. We occupied a different time zone in which hours and minutes were measured only from the time at which Lesley left for the fair. The only celebration that could hold any meaning would be the one we had when Lesley walked through the door and into my arms.

Elsie took me by the elbows and spoke gently but firmly to me. 'Listen, Ann, I'm sure she must be with friends. When she comes back please don't shout at her.'

And then they were gone. My sister's last words echoed in the sudden silence. Shout at her? Why should I shout at her? That stage was over. We shout at a child out of pity for ourselves and the worry it has caused us.

But I was already beyond that stage. The nightmares had already begun. I was already forming the pictures in my mind . . . the pictures which revealed to me where Lesley was. It was a woman – I was convinced it was a woman – a childless woman or a lonely woman whose child had died. Lesley would be all right, I was convinced. It was just a matter of getting her free before she became too upset. And of course it was a woman or at least something in the shape of a woman. Time would reveal the nature of she who held Lesley – that creature with her demented partner. Perhaps at that very moment when Elsie was advising me not to shout at Lesley a woman was shouting at her . . . in circumstances that sicken me to the depths of my being even now, 25 years later.

We drank coffee – lots of coffee. We watched the clock. We waited for a hesitant tap at the door. We had exhausted all possibilities as well as ourselves. We sat and waited for the next phase to begin, or our misery to end. I think the television was still on. I know the tea was still set on the table. Time had become twisted and distorted. The clock measured it but it didn't seem to move.

Ten thirty. Alan stood up. 'We're going to Mill Street, love. Never mind what time it is. This is ridiculous.' Ten forty-five, and we're rushing down those streets again. People staggering out of pubs. People laughing and calling out to each other. People whose lives are normal. They might as well have been on a different planet.

The same desk sergeant was on duty. His manner was

changed. On learning in no uncertain terms from Alan and me that Lesley had still not come home he became efficient and serious. We were led through to an interview room while a constable took over the desk duty. The system swung into operation . . . at last. After assurances from us that there had not been an argument and that we had already checked with friends and relatives he started to take Lesley's description.

Age?

Height?

Distinguishing marks?

Wearing?

Accompanied by?

Last seen by?

His face was serious and showed some concern at last. I began to complain that the lateness of the police reaction and the slight fall of snow would make things more difficult. I began to rail at the delay that had already occurred. We were ushered out into the station foyer. Alan and the sergeant were trying to calm me down.

'Leave it with us, Mrs Downey.'

And so we left it with them, unaware of the sleeping machine we had finally succeeded in stirring into life. We didn't know as we walked, physically and emotionally exhausted, once more towards Charnley Walk, of the telephones ringing in a hundred houses and flats all over Manchester and Cheshire. We couldn't know of the officers whose leave was being cancelled as we trudged once more up the steps to the flat. We had become a case – or rather, Lesley had. It was all beginning.

After Terry had been persuaded to go to bed and try to sleep I went to Lesley's room, put the light on and pulled the curtains right back. The light was on for Lesley, to steer her back to us in case she was lost and wandering in the darkness. We sat and waited for the rest of that long first night.

7

Sunday morning, 27 December 1964. All the streets were very quiet. People were having a leisurely lie-in after the festivities. We had not been to bed. We had huddled in the living room, drinking endless cups of coffee, waiting for the knock on the door that could bring either relief from our agony or confirmation of our worst fears. But no knock had come, only a grey dawn that hung heavy and dreary over the rooftops and streets of Miles Platting.

It was half-past eight and the children were still, thankfully, asleep. On an impulse we decided that we would try to clear our heads by taking a quick walk to the paper shop on Bradford Road. It was only a couple of minutes to the shop, which was quite busy with early-morning customers eager for cigarettes and newspapers after the Christmas shutdown. Our turn soon came. As we approached the counter the headlines on the neatly laid-out papers stared out at me. Somebody was talking to me.

'Have you heard about the little girl that's gone missing?'

The headlines screamed out at me. It was only what we knew, but seeing it set out in black and white seemed to make Lesley's disappearance more permanent, more total, more alarming. With my eyes still taking in the papers on the counter I heard myself answering weakly, 'It's my little girl . . . it's Lesley.'

We stood on the pavement and took in the large print across the width of the front page: LITTLE GIRL GOES MISSING FROM FAIRGROUND.

It was only later that we understood how the events of just the previous evening had become front-page national news by the next morning. Presumably somebody at Mill Street police station had given a tip-off to the press. We felt no resentment, as this was the type of case that needed maximum publicity in order for Lesley to be returned. Although we did not realise it at the time the long-running relationship that Alan and I were to have with the press had begun.

We hurried back to Charnley Walk, our eyes desperately scanning the pavements of Bradford Road and Tinsley Walk for any little girls who might be Lesley. Of course there were no little girls to be seen and Lesley was not waiting at home. We read the newspaper together. It told us nothing that we did not know already. My spirits rose somewhat as we read that all police leave for the rest of the Christmas period had been cancelled. At least we were being taken seriously now.

But the day dragged on and there was no further news. Some of the neighbours who had helped with our unofficial search the previous evening called in to see what help they could give. There was no help that anyone could give. All I wanted was assurance that Lesley Ann was safe and alive. Nobody could give me such hope. They could say the words but they were just words. Rose Travers, who shared the same landing, dropped in to see what she could do for Alan and the boys. I was losing control as the day went on and if it had not been for the kindliness of people such as Rose and Mrs White and Mr Johnson I do not know how we would have coped.

We couldn't bear to have the television or radio on. The frothy comedy and music programmes of the holiday period seemed somehow disrespectful to Lesley. Although I firmly believed that she was alive I couldn't stand anything that was bright or colourful around me. I was in mourning for her separation from us, not her death. She was being held by somebody and was unhappy, therefore I would not allow expressions of pleasure. That afternoon I changed into colours of mourning. It was a senseless gesture but one that satisfied some need I felt within me: a need to do something that would show my loss and longing. It was not for many, many months that I could wear bright colours.

Hour followed slow hour and steadily my hysteria grew. Alan struggled to calm me, to pacify the boys. He was a tower of strength, despite being badly affected by her disappearance himself. Many tears were shed that day. It was the beginning of a period of sorrow that is endless. Sorrow, confusion, worry and helplessness all combined to drive us deep within ourselves.

I think it was about five in the afternoon of that day of misery that there was a knock on the door. I can still recall the turmoil of the moment when Alan showed the two CID officers into the room. It was clear from the serious expressions on their faces that they were not the bearers of good news. 'Get it over with!' I thought to myself. 'Whatever it is, get it over with.' But they did not bring us any news. They had come for us.

'Mrs Downey, Mr West, would you accompany us to the police station? There are some questions that we have to ask you.'

We were both so distraught by this time that we didn't realise the significance of the words. They were words you normally hear in a film or play. We were so relieved in some ways that they had not come with news of something terrible that we didn't think straight. Hurriedly Alan made arrangements for Margaret Glennen, who had been a neighbour when we lived in Chorlton-on-Medlock, to come round from Tinsley Walk at the back of us to look after the boys and put Brett to bed if necessary. Their son was a good friend of Terry and she would be particularly suitable to help calm Lesley's very tearful brother.

On the brief journey in the unmarked CID car to Mill Street police station nothing was said. I wondered briefly why the questions they had to ask must be put to us at the station instead of at our flat. I told myself that it was the police being sensitive about upsetting the boys. Alan and I would soon learn that sensitivity was to form no part of the proceedings that evening.

After being asked to wait for a few moments in the front entrance hall we were soon led off separately to interview rooms somewhere in the depths of the building. There was the regulation uniformed police-woman and a detective. His tone was always calm and reasonable, his questions logical – but not very useful, it seemed to me. The information he was asking for had already been given the previous evening. And then it began to emerge . . . the innuendo, the suspicion.

'You read about these wicked stepfathers . . .'

I struggled to keep cool. This was crazy. Why were they wasting their time with this nonsense? I assured the detective that Alan might in practice be a stepfather to my children but there was nothing wicked about him. He was generous to a fault and never raised a finger to any of them. I felt my control going. I started to rail at him for wasting time when they should have been looking for Lesley. I accused the police of wasting hours by not listening to us on our first visit to the station.

'Do you or Alan have to smack the children very much? Did Alan ever smack Lesley?'

I became wild. It suddenly struck me that this madness was real. They were questioning *us*. We were being considered as possible murderers.

'Perhaps Lesley had been struck or beaten and ran away?'

'Nobody has ever had to slap Lesley. If you even talk sternly to her she collapses in tears.'

I wanted to tell them that Lesley wasn't that sort of girl, and we weren't that sort of family. Still he persevered, probing with his dirty questions, going back and checking on an answer and then carrying on with his suggestions.

'Was she a forward child?'

I couldn't understand what he was getting at.

'With Alan . . . was she forward?'

I wanted to be sick when the meaning became so horribly clear. I was trembling uncontrollably. I felt the kind hands of the policewoman gripping my shoulders, trying to calm me down. I cursed with rage and let him know what a foul mind he had. There was no let-up. If it wasn't Alan under the microscope as a possible child-molester or murderer then it was me as a suspected child-beater.

'How did Lesley feel towards Alan?'

'She loved him as a father. She played with him as a father. She tickled his feet and he would give her sixpence. She loved him. They were friends.' It suddenly struck me that I was talking about her in the past tense. 'She loves him. He is like a father to her . . . much better than her real father. He cares for her and loves her! Does that answer your sick question?'

On and on, over the same foul ground, hour after

hour. A break in the questions for a cup of tea. Cigarette smoke hung heavy in the small, bleak room. Are they stupid? Why are they persisting in these crazy half-accusations? Why don't they go and look for whoever really has got Lesley?

'Has Lesley run away before?'

'Lesley has not run away now. She has never run away. She has nothing to run away from. We love her! Can't you understand that?'

More trembling, more choking anger. The questions again and again. The minutes and the hours ticking away. Time being wasted.

'Christmas can be a very stressful time. Had there been arguments?'

How could I explain that this had started as the most wonderful Christmas we had ever had? For once there was a little money to spare thanks to Alan being with us; we were all together and the family was happy. I shook my head and sobbed incoherently.

'Come on now. That's enough for tonight.'

At last they had seen sense, or so I thought. I was not to know at the time that Alan was being put through much the same sort of thing in another room but with two detectives, grilling him mercilessly. Later I was to learn with revulsion that they had pressed the possibility of a sexual relationship even harder with Alan. How he controlled himself in the face of such filthy smears I will never know. On and on they had gone, trying either to get him to confess to murder or to get him to say that I had beaten Lesley or killed her in a domestic frenzy.

'Come clean. Have you done anything to the child?'

Alan looked each detective very coldly in the eyes and replied, 'Nothing at all.'

All this I was to discover later. For now I walked into the waiting area and saw with astonished fury my 8-year-old son Tommy being led from another room by a detective. He was in his pyjamas, covered by a black duffel coat, and was very white-faced and upset. It was nearly ten o'clock at night. The police had gone round to Charnley Walk and got Margaret Glennen to get him out of bed in order for them to question him at the station. Without permission from anyone, an 8-year-old boy had been taken from his bed and bundled into a police car to be asked upsetting questions for an hour concerning his missing sister and the behaviour of his mother and her 'boyfriend'.

'No way should you have interviewed that boy without my permission!' I told them.

I brushed aside their somewhat apologetic explanations about the need to establish or eradicate 'certain possibilties'. I realised that Tommy was an important witness in that he had been the last person to see Lesley at the fair, but surely there are more suitable ways of questioning a young lad? Finally Alan joined us and a very strained and distressed trio were taken back to Charnley Walk. The night had not yet ended.

The two CID officers who had accompanied us back home did not leave us at the door. I flopped on to the sofa with Tommy in my arms as Alan was made to lead the officers in a tour of the flat. Lesley's bedroom was first examined and the space under her bed checked. Next the boys' bedroom was searched, even though Brett was asleep in one of the beds. The wardrobe had to be opened for the detective to search its interior. I heard them on the landing next after our bedroom had been gone through.

'What's in this cupboard?'

I heard Alan's exasperated voice replying, 'It's an airing cupboard.'

'If you come clean now and tell us where she is it'll be easier on you.'

'We don't know where she is! That's why we came to you.'

Still the dogged, persistent voice of the detective, ignoring Alan's protests. 'It's possible you could hide a child in here.'

'It's an airing cupboard! It's got washing in it – see!'

I heard the sound of Alan piling the stacks of airing clothes on the landing and Terry sobbing from the chair by the fire. Would this nightmare never be over?

'Yes . . . well, the house seems to be clear.'

The front door opened, the cold night air creeping into the house.

'Where do you keep your rubbish?'

'There's a chute here. All the refuse from this landing goes down into a container – a sort of skip – below.'

I hugged Tommy closer to me. There was something obscene about the rubbish container being searched for Lesley's body. It defiled her in some way. It also insulted us, but that did not matter so much. Lesley was being treated as something that could be cast away, abandoned as useless, discarded.

Finally, after over an hour of upsetting and time-wasting searching, they left. Alan told me that they had apologised in their own way. They had thanked us for our help and explained that this was what they had to do. I shook my head. It was disgusting. In the absence of any other line of enquiry they had assumed us guilty until circumstances proved us innocent. They had assumed we were child-beaters, child-molesters, child-killers. A cold fury ran through me. In my head I know that the police have to check all avenues of possibility but in my heart I feel that there must be more diplomatic ways of treating parents in such a situation. Perhaps the police have to make themselves hard to cope with the distressing cases they meet each week but they must know that parents are at their most vulnerable at such times. A child has gone missing, their lives are in turmoil . . . Is it really necessary for the police to suggest the terrible things they did to Alan and to me?

And so began another night of waiting. There were to be many more – so many more – when hopes for the future and memories of the past combined to cheat us out of sleep. All through this second night Alan and I sat and stared at one another in horrified silence.

A door had been pushed open, and through it a sordid and vicious world was half-revealed to us. It was a world where loving people could be accused of unspeakable and sordid crimes against the innocence of children. It was a world of perverted vicousness where there was no survival for the meek.

I held Tommy close to me and saw Alan's haunted face as he chain-smoked, gazing at a blank wall with unseeing eyes. I knew that he had seen through that door, perhaps been pushed by the hours of questioning towards the threshold for a closer look. The hours limped by and still we waited, shedding silent tears as we both sensed, without knowing, that Lesley was part of that terrible world beyond the door. Our lost innocent was calling to us and we were powerless to hold out a hand.

8

Weeks and months of waiting. A terrible January dragged its way into a worse February. Month followed month with only hope to make life endurable. The light burned brightly day and night in Lesley's bedroom, but my heart held nothing but agony and a dark dread that she was being ill-treated by whoever was ·holding her prisoner. Looking back on those agonising ten months it seems ironic that I saw the very best but also the very worst in human nature. Alan, the children, Harold Ford and his congregation, neighbours and friends were absolutely selfless in their efforts to keep me sane and hanging on to the desperate hope that kept me alive. Journalists, cranks and charlatans seemed to conspire to drive me and the rest of the family to distraction.

I was on eight or nine full-strength sedatives a day

throughout that period, so my memory of events is somewhat hazy. I was going through the motions of living and each slow day dawned only to die in another twilight of disappointment. I do remember the afternoon in January when Alan and I received a message that Mary Waugh, who ran a small grocer's shop on Bradford Road, wanted to see us. We hurried through the grey streets with Brett holding tightly on to our hands to see what had happened. Perhaps there had been a sighting of Lesley. We were breathless by the time we got there.

Mary took us into the back of her shop and explained what she had done. Together with some of the neighbours in the district she had organsied a collection. They had raised, in the space of a few days, the sum of £100. She explained that they were having posters printed with Lesley's photograph on them and distributing them all over the Manchester area. Naturally Alan and I were in tears at such kindness. A hundred pounds was, in those days, a considerable amount of money, and the area was by no means a wealthy one. It was clear that people had dug very deep indeed into their pockets. Within days it was not possible to walk in any area of Manchester without seeing Lesley's face staring from the hundreds of posters that appeared in shops, pubs, libraries and cafés. She stirred a city's conscience and kept my hope alive.

So many faces and names emerge from that terrible time and some disappeared. My neighbour Mary Clark, who should have accompanied Lesley and her own daughter to the fair on that fateful night, suddenly moved out of the area. Perhaps it was the strain of living in a street that had suddenly become busy day and night with police, press and cranks as well as those who came to offer impossible comfort. Some of the other neighbours suggested it was guilt at not going with the kids to the fair. Who can say?

Father de Clerk, a Belgian Roman Catholic priest in the locality, was a wonderful distracation to Alan and the boys on his weekly visit. Although we had told him that we attended the Methodist church he insisted that we were all brothers and sisters before God and continued to visit regularly. He was a real comedian and very much a man of the world who liked a joke and a drink as well as a flutter on the horses. He was always giving Alan tips for horses that couldn't fail to win and would make us a fortune. If we'd had any spare cash we might have taken up some of his suggestions. He was clearly a believer in the principle that those who are suffering should be distracted. There is always a time for those who will sit and weep with you, but Father de Clerk firmly adopted a 'laughter is the best medicine' approach. I don't think I ever saw him sit down normally in a chair or sofa, for example. He would leap over the back and flop into a seat as if he were hopping on to the back of one of those horses he was always recommending Alan to put a shilling on. We lost touch with him when we moved to Hattersley. He was a good man.

Another man of the church and one to whom we

became deeply indebted was Harold Ford, who had only recently become the Methodist minister in charge of Holy Trinity Church which served the local area. In his forties, with a wife and two teenage children, he constantly tried to bring us some sort of consolation for Lesley's disappearance. He would ask Alan what hymn he would like sung at the services, and the choir of which Lesley Ann had been a member would always oblige. It was usually 'The Coming of the Lord'. When the memories and press torments became too much and we asked the council to move us it seemed that we would lose touch with Holy Trinity and the kind leader of its flock. To go from the new overspill estate at Hattersley to Holy Trinity meant a walk, followed by a bus ride and then another walk. It started to become too much to do this every week and we made our apologies one Sunday in August.

'You'll be able to get to church,' he quietly assured us.

Next Sunday we found one of the congregation waiting outside for us in his car. 'How typical,' I remember thinking. 'How kind of the Reverend Harold Ford to go out of his way to arrange a lift.' His kindness didn't end there, however. We received a message at the end of the service that we were invited to Sunday lunch with his family. Walking with Harold and his wife towards his house after the service Alan commented that he must have visitors as there was a car parked outside the house in the road. But nobody appeared to be around.

'I said you would be able to get to church even though you are out at Hattersley. It's yours.'

The kids nearly went berserk with excitement. Alan looked astonished and I clung to his arm in confusion.

'It's a Ford Popular, Dad!' shouted Terry. 'It's in great condition. Can we go for a drive now?'

Alan protested that we couldn't accept such a gift, but he insisted and I cried tears of gratitude for Harold Ford's impetuous generosity. It was quietly explained to us that he believed we had suffered enough so far, and he himself joked that he didn't want to lose members of his congregation so early in his ministry at Holy Trinity; besides, we would need transport for our frequent visits to the police station and to follow up alleged sightings of Lesley. I will never forget the quiet concern and self-sacrifice of Harold Ford – a true Christian friend.

But Lesley was still missing, and even if we had won the football pools it would not have compensated in any way for the absence of our shy and loving daughter. I'm not sure if it's amusing or simply a sad comment on our finances by the summer of 1965, but driving back to Hattersley that afternoon in our 'new' car we ran short of petrol. The only money we had between us was a lucky silver shilling that we kept as a sort of good luck token, not that it seemed to have brought us much luck lately. With a shilling's worth of petrol in the tank we limped home to Bowden Close to wait as always for an end to the terrible purgatory.

But the end of the waiting was a long time coming. It never struck me in those long months that the end might not be what we all desired; that it would be the commencement of a far greater and far longer horror.

We lived from one featureless day to the next, each of us coping in our individual way. Of the three boys it was probably Terry who was most devastated by Lelsey's disappearance. One Sunday when we still lived at Charnley Walk we were leaving for church when Terry asked us to wait for a moment as we were leaving the flat. There were the usual press photographers hanging around for something to snap and fill a few inchs of column space. We watched curiously as Terry stuck a note to the door. Although only fourteen he was learning to use the press as they had used us. The note read: LESLEY IS MY SISTER – DON'T HURT HER – WE MISS HER SO MUCH – IF SOMEONE'S KIDNAPPED HER – LET US KNOW – PLEASE.

Both Alan and I realised at that moment that he was still blaming himself for not having gone to the fair and protecting his little sister.

Unfortunately not everybody was as sympathetic to our loss. We threw away the crank letters from pathetic creatures with sick minds as soon as we got them. Some will stay in my mind forever. I suppose that I should feel pity for the twisted minds that can write the filth and obscenity that came through our letter-box. I wish I could claim to be so forgiving. One of the stranger notes raved on about us being lucky we still had children left; it concluded: 'I lost my leg in the war, so what are you complaining about?' The letters were usually unsigned.

Others came in person and played their sick games to raise our hopes and then dash them to the ground. Some were probably well-meaning, others mentally deranged.

Most days brought us some apparent news of Lesley or her possible whereabouts. Of course, each bringer of news was mistaken, but only with hindsight could that be said. At the time each clue or sighting had to be followed up. Anything was better than not knowing.

One of the more well-meaning and possibly more accurate contributors to our search for Lesley was the Dutch clairvoyant Emile Croiset. He had a track record of assisting the police in searches for missing persons and volunteered his services about six weeks after the terrible Christmas. Alan and I went to Mill Street police station where the Dutchman was in the process of trying to get a sense of the events of 26 December. After a great deal of concentration he came out with the words that first undermined my faith in Lesley's survival. 'I can see the body of a child in a field area . . . She put up a struggle . . . There are four people . . . There is water . . . There is a motorbike.'

Later that day the police took Croiset and ourselves to Hulme Hall Lane and the site of the fair. He walked around a couple of times and then pointed to a road that led to the east. The police began to take notes.

'There is a road . . . it divides at a fork . . . There is a cemetery . . . the people who have taken the little girl have gone on the low road.'

At the time it meant little to us. It seemed to give the police little to go on either. I refused to believe that Lesley was not still alive. I refused to listen to this Dutchman and his inspired ramblings. When the trial brought out the events of that grim Boxing Day it seemed that Croiset might have been more accurate than any of us could have imagined.

'The people who have taken the little girl have gone on the low road.' The low road in question led eventually to Hattersley. It is precisely the route that Brady and Hindley would have taken Lesley after they abducted her at the fair. It was at Hindley's grandmother's house in Hattersley that Lesley was tortured, photographed, tape-recorded and killed. It was at the same house in Hattersley, a few months later, that Edward Evans would be hacked to death and Brady and Hindley arrested.

'The body of a child in a field area.' It was in a shallow grave in the bleak fields of Saddleworth Moor that Lesley was found the following October. It was in the same notorious fields that John Kilbride and eventually Pauline Reade were discovered. Only Brady and Hindley know how many more innocent victims of their perverted games lie waiting for a final resting-place.

'There are four people.' With the arrest of the two sadists, Brady and Hindley, it may seem that this vision is totally irrelevant. Claims made by Brady at the trial make Croiset's words strangely significant. He insisted that two men brought Lesley to the house in Hattersley for the purpose of taking pornographic photographs. He even insisted that Lesley was still alive when she was handed back to the two men that he refused to name. Myra Hindley's brother-in-law, Dave Smith, had been present in that same house when Edward Evans was hacked to death. Nobody really knows how close

Smith's relationship was with his sick sister-in-law and her perverted lover. Had he been there when Lesley was so grossly abused and killed ten months previously? He turned Queen's Evidence to help the prosecution convict Brady and Hindley. His own record is not a good one: after the events of 1964 and 1965 he was convicted of assault.

'There is a motorbike.' Ian Brady had used a motorbike. The only driving licence he had was for a motorbike. The mini-van used by the grotesque couple for picking up youngsters and later taking their bodies to their cruel graves on the moor was always driven by Hindley.

Emile Croiset may have been closer than anyone realised to 'seeing' what had happened that grim December day six weeks previously. His visions led to nothing tangible and we returned to our long ordeal of waiting. We were not short of suggestions as to where Lesley might be. Some people were obviously after the reward money that our poster offered. Others were simply satisfying whatever weird craving they had to cause yet further misery to a bewildered mother and family.

One man called to say that he had recently seen Lesley with a young couple on a bus at Bellevue. Of course he hadn't noted the number of the bus. He was typical of a certain type of crank with which we had to deal. Another contacted us to say that Lesley had been seen with a couple in Belgium. This time there was a car registration number. Interpol were contacted but eventually it turned out to be a young girl being taken to a convent. Only increased doses of sedatives allowed me to cope with the constant pattern of raised hopes followed by disappointment and dejection.

I suppose it was our increased desperation that stopped us from recognising that the lady who called claiming to be a clairvoyant was nothing more than a drunken and confused old woman. She managed to convince us that a vision had shown her Lesley being buried in a patch of waste ground just off Deansgate in the centre of Manchester. Alan and my friend Mary Glennen went with me in the evening to investigate. On our hands and knees we dug with bare hands amongst the broken bricks and glass and waste, searching for Lesley, desperate to put an end to the everlasting nightmare. It was a harrowing and soul-destroying evening. We told ourselves that the lack of success at least meant that Lesley was still alive. Such were the straws we invented to cling to. With bleeding fingers and covered in dirt we returned to our long vigil.

The move to Bowden Close on the large overspill housing development at Hattersley was a reaction to the cruel memories and press harassment. We had hoped that somehow going there would make the waiting more bearable. The council had generously given us a choice of location. Hattersley, on the Cheshire side of Manchester, seemed an ideal place to be with Alan and the boys, leaving the worst of the memories behind. It was to be the place where we could renew our hopes and dreams of Lesley's return. It was not until October and the capture of Hindley and Brady at the house on Wardle Brook Avenue where they had staged their debauched rituals of death that we realised we had moved closer to the scene of the nightmare itself. We had become distant, unknowing neighbours of Lesley's perverted killers. Thank God we were spared that knowledge. If we had known, it is more than possible that there would have been two more murders in Hattersley.

9

17 October 1965. From the depths of drug-induced sleep I felt Alan getting out of bed. I turned over and tried to shut out the mocking voices and Lesley's whispered calls for help. Alan was always a light sleeper, more so since Christmas. I struggled to lose myself in the pit of unconsciousness and hide from the taunting nightmares that always hovered on the edges of sleep. The pills were still strong in my bloodstream and I felt again the spiralling fall into the blackness. But there was still a voice calling. I tried to push my face deeper into the pillows, moaning softly to myself. If the pills weren't going to work what hope was there? The voice became clearer. Perhaps another pill would help me steal another hour or so of escape.

'What the hell . . . what the hell's going on?'

I stirred and rolled on to my back, eyes wide open, staring at the merciful blankness of the ceiling. It was Alan's voice. Where was he? He had got out of bed, hadn't he? I tried to clear my head. The drugs were cruel, befuddling me sufficiently to confuse but denying me the escape of sleep. I shifted myself higher in the bed to try to gain some sort of consciousness. Alan was standing at the window peering into the street below. I struggled to focus my eyes in the half-light of the room. A thin grey light filtered through the net of the curtains; Alan's silhouette was rigid and unmoving, staring intently into the cruel dawn of the street.

A wild hope stirred in my heart for a moment. Perhaps . . .? And the hope died as soon as it was born. If it had been her he would have been down the stairs and into the street to sweep her into his arms. A sort of reality returned.

'What is it, love? What's wrong?'

He didn't answer but turned and looked at me with an expression of silent despair I will never forget. I lay for a moment and stared back at him. I think now that I knew at that moment . . . knew that the waiting was over and the real nightmare was beginning.

'It's the press, Ann. The close is full of them.'

His voice was expressionless and flat. It was the voice of a man from whom all hope and possibility of joy had been drained. I struggled from under the suffocating blankets and stumbled to join him at the window. I needed to see, to be sure that he was not hallucinating, to feel the reality of him next to me. He put an arm out to comfort me or perhaps to support me. I fought to make my eyes focus through the net of the curtains at the window. Lights were on in all the windows on the opposite side of the close. Here and there faces were looking down into the street. I looked down myself and gave a gasp of dismay. At least a dozen cars were parked haphazardly on the pavements and across the play area. Groups of people in twos and threes were huddled in the early-morning cold, their breath rising into the chill winter air. Faces were turned upwards, staring at our windows. Alan held me tighter as I froze. Not again . . . please God, not the media again . . . not the media and what their presence there in the close must mean.

The scene below began to blur as the tears welled up into my eyes. Cameramen were swarming on the grassy bank at the end of the cul-de-sac, where their power cables twisted and twined towards television vans parked up on the pavements and in driveways. Press photographers were jostling against the walls and hedges of the normally quiet road which had been our refuge. Suddenly I felt my heart pumping madly. Icy water surged in my stomach and my legs gave way. As I slumped to the floor I heard myself whispering hoarsely, 'It's Lesley . . . the body on the moor . . . it's our Lesley!'

I must have passed out. The next thing I can recall is sitting on the edge of the bed with Alan on his knees in front of me. His voice came to me distantly.

'Take it easy, darling. Don't jump to conclusions. It doesn't mean it's our Lesley. They could be here for anything. Please, love.'

His voice was still flat and there was no conviction in his tone. I rocked silently in his arms. Not after last night, not after the panic and the phone calls and the cruel hope. I closed my eyes and the scenes of short hours ago ran through my brain like some speeded-up film. A television newsflash had interrupted the programme we were half-watching.

'We interrupt this programme with news that is coming in from our Manchester studio. Police have discovered the body of a child in a shallow grave on Saddleworth Moor near Manchester. There are no further details but investigating officers say an identification will be made shortly. Any further information will be given in our news summary at the end of this programme.'

Alan had struggled to calm my mounting hysteria. Bitter bile rose in my throat. Words were repeated like a crazy prayer: 'Oh God, not my Lesley – not Lesley – please God – let it not be Lesley.' Alan's arms were round me, trying to soothe me, trying to stop my panic from breaking out once more.

'It can't be her, Ann! The police would have contacted us first before allowing a newsflash. It's like you said – like you've always said.'

For a moment I allowed myself the comfort of the belief that for nine long months had kept me going . . . kept both of us going. Lesley trapped in the house of some old woman demented by loneliness. Lesley miserable but safe in the imprisoning love of some childless woman. Lesley waiting until an opportunity arose to escape and run back home to us.

'Oh God, Alan. I've got to get to a phone!'

The picture in my mind didn't seem so secure any more. It was shaking and going out of focus, being crumpled by a bland BBC voice saying something about the body of a child in a shallow grave. I was on my feet and standing helpless at the door of the room. I turned and looked at Alan. His face was white and tears were in his eyes. He nodded. I was only in my dress and a silly pair of bedroom slippers but I didn't feel the damp of the pavements as we ran, hand in hand, through the sodium-lit streets of the estate. It was only four streets to get to the phone that Joan, a neighbour, let us use. I was breathless and Alan rang the doorbell while I stood impatiently by, every nerve-end jangling. Joan stood in the doorway for a moment. No words. The sound of a television in the background. A nod of the head that said everything. Fingers fumbling at the too-familiar number. A mis-dial. Another try. Alan's hand on my shoulder in the cramped hall. 'Easy, take it easy. Everything's going to be OK.' My words came out in a garbled rush: 'Is it Lesley on the moor? Is Lesley dead? Please tell me – I've got to know. Please tell me the truth. Is it her? Please!' a pause, a terrible pause and then, 'No, Mrs Downey. The body is not Lesley Ann. It is the body of a boy.' A moment of blissful calm and then more panic: 'Please don't lie to me. If it is Lesley, please, please tell me.' The voice at the other end of the phone was very calm and reassuring: 'Stop crying, Mrs Downey. Go home, get some sleep. Stop worrying. I can assure you that the body that has been found is that of a young lad.' The phone hanging in my hand and Alan replacing it gently. Burying my head in Alan's chest and muttering over and over again, 'Thank God, thank God.' Finally I looked up at Alan: 'It's not my little girl, Alan. Oh Alan, it's not her.' Joan stood in the open door of the living room with a relieved smile on her face. The three of us clung tightly together in the narrow hall as waves of relief broke over us.

Walking back through the drizzle to the house, hand in hand, we got soaked but didn't care. Lesley was still alive. It was all so real I could almost feel her arms round me and the gentle sound of her voice whispering in my ears.

The sound of two firm raps on the door below hurled me into the reality of that grotesque dawn. Alan grabbed his dressing-gown and pausing only to give my shoulder a gentle squeeze went downstairs. I pulled on my thin housecoat and followed him down. I went and sat shivering in the cold of the living room and listened to Alan unlocking the door.

'May we come in, please?'

The voices were firm but polite . . . too polite. I could feel my hands shaking but dared not move to get the tranquillisers that eased the agony of each bleak morning. Two tall plain-clothes policemen came quietly into the room with Alan behind them. The sound of voices outside and the pop of flashbulbs made their terrible words unnecessary. They looked from me to Alan and then back to me. They seemed awkward and although their age suggested they were long-serving members of the force they hesitated with what I can only call embarrassment. Finally the older man coughed and stepped towards me.

'Mrs Downey . . .' He stopped and after a short pause started again.

'Mrs Downey, we hate to do this but it's our job.' He turned for a moment and looked at his colleague as if for support. The younger man looked down at the floor. Summoning up some sort of final courage he forced out the prepared but fatal words.

'Mrs Downey, it is our sad duty to ask you to come down to the mortuary with us to make a formal identification.'

There was a long silence. Even the voices and noise of cars outside seemed to die. I looked up at the police officer and then at Alan. There were tears in the eyes of both men. I began to shake all over. The room started to spin wildly out of control. I closed my eyes and forced some sort of order into this madness.

'But last night . . . the telephone call. They said it wasn't my Lesley. You said it was a little boy.' I could hear my own voice pleading, begging for someone to say that it was all a mistake. But as I spoke I knew that the mistake was mine. I knew but refused to accept the reality of the nightmare. Even the police seemed to want to clutch at straws.

'It may not be Lesley. It might be someone else. We just can't be sure.'

There was another short pause and then the younger

officer dealt the body blow.

'We need you to come and look at the clothes the little girl was wearing . . . to see if you can identify them. They might belong to someone else.'

I remember moaning quietly to myself and rocking to and fro. Alan came and sat next to me as the policemen shuffled rather awkwardly in their discomfort. I knew then that what I was in for was more than just an identification of somebody's clothes. The police had a detailed description of what she had been wearing. I was going to be taken to see Lesley's clothes . . . and I was going to be forced to see what for ten months I had forced deep into the blackness of my terrified imagination.

'Go and get dressed, love. It's cold. We'd better see about getting a neighbour to look after the kids while you're both away.' He nodded to the younger officer who left the room. 'It won't take long.'

His professionalism returned. He had done what for him was the difficult part. For Alan and me it was just starting.

I found myself in the bedroom without knowing how I had got there. Movements became involuntary and distanced. My brain seemed numb although tears ran constantly down my face. Alan was zipping me into one of my black dresses. My fingers wouldn't work. Alan put his hands on my shoulders but I moved toward the landing and the stairs. I was being drawn to that place . . . that place that held the death of my hope and my life. A neighbour was sitting on the sofa in the living room with her arm round Terry. She looked up with confusion in her eyes. Terry pulled himself away from her and ran to me, flinging his arms round me and burying his face in my shoulder.

'It's not going to be Lesley, Mum. No one would hurt her. She's too . . .' He broke down sobbing and I cupped his face in my shaking hands and kissed him. Then we walked to the door.

As the senior police officer opened the door there was an explosion of flashbulbs and shouted questions and mircrophones being pushed into my face. We froze for a second and then Alan tried to guide me forward to the waiting unmarked police car. At a signal the two policemen in the car jumped out and tried to elbow their way through the mob of journalists who were probing at us with their lenses and demands and unheard questions. Finally we were both bundled into the back seat, squeezed in with one of the officers.

'Let's get out of here – fast!' he commanded, and with a screech of tyres and another flurry of flashbulbs aimed at the car interior we were away. We were dimly aware of figures running and the sound of car engines starting up but soon we were clear of the pursuing horde, driving at high speed down some back road. The driver checked for following press cars in his mirror a couple of times and our eyes met. He looked away quickly.

Alan held me tight and the senior officer who was on my other side squeezed my hand reassuringly. He was not successful.

'Don't keep crying, love,' said Alan. 'Dry your eyes.

Try to be brave. We don't know that it's Lesley yet.'

How this last word terrified me. 'Yet' . . . even Alan knew what must be in store for us.

We were out of Hattersley and swinging on to the main road in Uppermill. They were waiting – more of them with their cameras and questions and obscene microphones. The car swerved into the car park at the rear of the mortuary and pulled up with a screech of tyres. Suddenly the officer who had tried to reassure me was flinging open the door and pulling me after him.

'Come on, love. Don't stop for anybody!'

He was pulling off his coat and before I could do anything he had flung it over my head. I could hear Alan protesting and then my arm was gripped firmly. I was being half-dragged, half-guided across the car park. I felt like a criminal. I could hear the shouted questions of reporters from all around.

'Why are you here, Mrs Downey?'

'What have the police told you?'

'Do you think it will be Lesley, Mrs Downey?'

'How do you feel, Mrs Downey?'

I stumbled up some steps and then we were inside. The coat was removed from my head and Alan was grabbing my hand.

'Are you all right, love?'

I nodded dumbly. So long as Alan was with me I could cope. I heard the door from the car park being bolted and was suddenly aware of Alan being led to one side by one of the officers.

'I'm sorry, Mrs Downey, but we can't let him inside

with you. He's not a relative, you see. He has to stay here.'

'But –'

'I'm sorry – it's regulations. We'd like to but there it is.'

I stared dumbly at Alan. It was unbelievable. After all his concern for all those months, after all the tears and misery we had shared together . . . not a relative? It was one of the sicker jokes of a day that had not even begun to throw its worst at us. I knew there was no use in arguing. We'd had enough experience of police methods by now to know of 'regulations' and how 'doing things by the book' was almost a police fetish. I was guided deeper into that terrible place, leaving Alan with a uniformed constable who was ordered to keep the media mob outside.

I was not prepared, but then there is no possible preparation for what lay beyond the next door. It took my eyes a few seconds to adjust to the light and then I saw the table a few steps away. With the officer holding my arm I approached. There were clothes laid out on the surface of the table – Lesley's clothes.

'Oh no! Oh my God, no! Not my little girl . . .'

A white blouse, a pair of trews, a pink cardigan, white Aertex knickers and vest to match, blue woollen coat with collar of white and blue piping, ankle-length socks . . . and the sweet, putrid stench of decay. I doubled up and vomited convulsively over the stone floor of the mortuary. This was all wrong. This was all horribly, monstrously wrong. Not Lesley . . . not quiet, sweet, loving Lesley . . . not this.

I was being supported and my mouth was being dabbed

at with a handkerchief. The officer said nothing, but what was there to say? His gesture was one of kindness and dignity in a place that stripped such qualities away with slabs and tables and card indexes. I looked again. At one side, separate from the crumpled clothing, lay a small blue shoe on its own. For a moment fury made me tremble and I wanted to lash out, to scream, to rage against fate or chance or whatever had led to this. The single shoe seemed a cruel symbol of the loneliness that Lesley had suffered out there on the moors. I did not then know of the suffering to which she had been subjected before she was casually disposed of in that shallow grave.

Next to the shoe lay the beads. A cheap matching necklace and bracelet of white, plastic beads together with a metal ring with a piece of white plastic glued to the centre: cheap fairground prizes which to Lesley had been more precious than gold. They had been a gift to her from Terry who had won them from a shooting gallery at the fair. He had left them on her dressing-table one night while she was asleep and the next morning they were the first thing she saw when she awoke. It had been typical of the close and loving relationship they had both enjoyed. Now they were just cheap trinkets on a table in a mortuary. I felt cold rage running once more through my veins.

I was being led deeper into the place. There were more doors. There was a new smell to assault the senses; a smell of rubber and formaldehyde. The room was cold even for October. My eyes took in a stainless steel sink on one wall, flaking plaster and a low ceiling. There was a table. The table was three or four steps from the door.

A hand was at my elbow and I was being led forward. My first reaction may seem a strange one. It was thankfulness that somebody had protected Lesley's modesty at least. A green sheet covered the little body from stomach to feet. For some reason the sheet had been drawn up to hide the right-hand side of her torso and face. It was only later that my imagination allowed itself to consider the reasons for such discretion.

She looked beautiful. She seemed to be asleep. Her dark, curly hair spilled out over the protective sheet. I winced as I saw the swelling round her lips. It was as if she had bitten hard on them. This was the only visible sign of the obscene ordeal to which we were later to learn she had been subjected, or at any rate the only sign that was to be revealed to me.

'Oh Lesley . . .' I murmured, reaching out to touch the hair which had fallen across her pale brow. A hand pulled back my arm.

'No. You mustn't touch her. We'd love to be allowed to let you but we can't.'

This couldn't be happening. I stared at the officer in bewilderment for a moment. Not after all this time. . .surely I was not to be denied a last contact with the dead body of my only daughter? The enormous finality and horror finally hit me. My stomach heaved and I stumbled over to the sink in an agony of dry retching. I felt the officer behind me and his hand on the small of my back. His other hand massaged my stomach to try to take the pain away. I remembered my father doing that when I was a girl . . . when I was Lesley's age. I nodded dumbly in gratitude.

Nobody asked me if it was Lesley. There was no need. It was obvious. A second policeman was at my side pouring a large measure of brandy. He took my hand and put the glass in it. I gagged and vomited again. He made me take some more and this time the powerful spirit stayed down.

'Come on, love. It's time to go,' said the elder officer, taking my arm and trying to draw me towards the door. It was all too sudden, too soon.

'No! Please let me stay. Let me look at her once more.'

He continued to lead me away.

'Please. Just once more?'

He stood aside and let me walk to the slab where Lesley lay so silently. She had always been a quiet girl but this silent stillness was something I had not experienced before. This was the absolute and final stillness of death. My Lesley was dead. I knew it now. I knew it but could not accept it.

I stood for a moment and imagined the blue eyes resting behind the closed lids. I stared at the green sheet that covered the right side of her head and started to imagine what reason there might be for it.

'Oh Lesley . . .'

I bent to kiss her bruised lips goodbye but a hand on my shoulder stopped me.

'Can I have a lock of her hair, then?' I begged.

His eyes looked down at the floor in what I took to be shame. He slowly shook his head. A physical pain doubled me up and I fell to my knees and retched once more on the floor at the side of Lesley.

Strong arms were half-supporting, half-dragging me towards the door. I twisted round in desperation for a last glimpse of my Lesley. The green sheet had already been drawn over her face. I was too late. I would never see Lesley again. Alan rushed to me and folded me in his arms. We clung together, a small island of quiet despair in a sea of noise that was beginning to be heard from outside. We were allowed a few moments for our quiet tears. Alan tried to wipe my cheeks with the back of his hand.

'Come on. Let's get you both out of here and back home.'

Our moment was over. Hands were guiding us to the door. A coat was thrown over my head again and again Alan protested. There were steps and shouting and jostling. Once more we ran the gauntlet of flashbulbs and the inane questions being called from all sides.

'Was it Lesley?'

'Was it your daugher?'

'What can you tell us?'

'How do you feel?'

That question again. The ultimate obscene question: the question that attempts to rape you of your deepest inner sorrow. I wanted to shout, 'I feel a deep longing to be dead. I feel I want to kill those who are responsible for that body on a cold slab. I feel I want to take your cameras and your microphones and . . . ' But I said nothing.

The car again. The same hazy October light. The same pointless high-speed drive down lanes and back streets. More photographers and reporters swarming all over the garden and the pavements round the house. The coat again – flung over my head as if I were a criminal being taken for questioning. All so meaningless. . .all so stupid. What did it matter now? What did anything matter?

Terry was in the hall, expectant, hoping against hope. He looked into my eyes and he knew. He came into my arms and the tears flooded out.

'It's my fault, Mum,' he sobbed. 'It's all my fault. I shouldn't have let Lesley go by herself. I should have been with her. I let her down. I should have protected her. I let her down!'

All the rage and guilt came spilling out. All the rage and the guilt and the grief. How could I explain to him? How could I tell him about a world that contains within it monsters and psychopaths? I held him to my breast and prayed that tears and time would wash the rage and guilt from his heart.

Alan took the burden of explaining to Tommy and Brett that they would never see their sister again. He took them into the living room, sat them on his knee and told them that Lesley had gone to Heaven and was with the angels. They asked if she was happy in heaven and with tears in his eyes Alan assured them that she was. This simple story seemed to satisfy them and when a kind neighbour took them for the afternoon they went without tears or visible signs of having been harmed by the chaos that had taken over our lives.

The rest of that terrible Sunday was a constant procession of relatives, neighbours and friends coming to offer their condolences and help. There was no help that they could give. Nothing they could say or do would wipe away the cruel image that was burnt into my memory. . .the picture of a little girl lying still on a cold slab in a mortuary.

The doctor came later in the afternoon and insisted on giving me a heavy sedative. Alan led me upstairs and put me to bed. I was already groggy with the drug that was running through my system. I saw him pulling the curtains to and thanked him for this gesture of respect for Lesley. He nodded and came and sat on the bed. I later learned that he had been forced to draw all the curtains in the house as photographers had been swarming around for hours tying to get their front-page 'picture of grief'. We were under siege.

I lay and felt waves of darkness sweeping over me. For a moment Lesley's face remained before me with the eyes closed forever. . .and then she was gone.

10

Alan already knew about the tape and photographs but had done his best to keep from me the enduring evidence of the iniquities Brady and Hindley had committed against Lesley. He had been told, unofficially, of their existence by a desk sergeant at Hyde police station when he went to collect Lesley's possessions. Desperate to protect me from further anguish he had carried the secret knowledge around with him for days, hoping somehow that I would not be tortured further. Surely Lesley's death was enough?

I learned later of the two battered brown suitcases recovered from the left luggage office of Central Station – the suitcases containing their everlasting nightmares which, when they saw the light of day, would condemn Brady and Hindley as the monsters they are. On that

Saturday afternoon I was ignorant of their existence, half-dozing on the sofa in the living room waiting for the third Valium of the day to take effect.

I think I remember the knock on the door. I remember the apologetic expression on the face of the detective that Alan ushered reluctantly into the room. I will never forget, however hard I try, the contents of the buff folder he carried under his arm. At that moment he was simply another officer coming to tie up some administrative loose ends. I think I was vaguely irritated that he was intruding on the Valium haze into which I was about to slip.

'Ann, love, I have something I must show you.'

For a second or so it meant nothing. I sat in my innocent misery and wondered what he was talking about. I looked to Alan for some sort of clue. His eyes showed nothing but pain. The Valium mist was stripped away.

'What is it?'

He took the buff folder from under his arm. Although I hadn't a clue what it contained I felt my nerves setting off alarms all over my body. My hand began to shake and I gripped it with my other hand.

'I have some photographs I must show you. We know they're Lesley but we have to have a formal identification.'

Alan stepped between the officer and me.

'Let me do it. I can tell you whether it's Lesley or not,' he pleaded. I could hear the panic in his voice. 'Don't show them to Ann. She's already gone through enough.'

Even then I did not realise the significance of Alan's concern. I did not realise the depths to which human beings can sink. My naivety was short-lived.

'Just show them to me!' Alan begged.

'I'm sorry but we don't have any choice. Lesley's mother has to make formal identification of her daughter.' His voice had become official. There was silence for a moment in the room and then the tone of the officer's voice softened. 'Believe me . . . if there was any other way . . .' He came a step towards me and taking my hand gave it a squeeze. 'We've tried to make it as easy as possible, love. We've selected two that aren't so bad.'

He opened the folder, took out two Polaroid colour photographs and placed them in my unwilling hand. I couldn't look down at them. I couldn't force my eyes to take witness of whatever it was that had happened to my Lesley. I still had no knowledge of those hours she had been with Brady and Hindley but something was beginning to tell me that these photographs were not for a mother's eyes.

'Please look. You've got to,' said the policeman with some distress in his voice.

And so I looked down at my lap. For no more than a couple of seconds I stared at the contradictory horrors that were recorded forever in the glossy colours of the photograph. I snapped my eyes shut and then fell forward to the floor screaming continuously and kicking out like a wounded animal. I put my hands desperately over my closed eyes but still the foul image burned in my brain.

Lesley . . . naked, bound and gagged with a scarf that

had been viciously forced into her mouth and tied tight at the back of her neck with a savage jerk. Lesley . . . pale and naked on a candlewick bedspread with her hands together in desperate prayer. Lesley . . . her hands tied together by sick people who revelled in her humiliation.

The second image swam behind my tight shut eyes and superimposed itself over the first horror. Lesley . . . bent double over a chair. Lesley still naked, bound and gagged. I screamed louder and louder, trying to make the images go away. But the expression of terror in Lesley's bulging eyes remained in sharp focus, imprinted on my mind. Lesley . . . who had never experienced a hand raised in anger at any time in her short life.

My face was being slapped. 'Yes, hurt me,' I thought for a moment. 'Hurt me instead of Lesley.' My face was slapped again. I opened my eyes and Alan and the policeman were bending over me. I sat on the floor, holding my knees to try to stop the terrible shaking that had overcome my body. The question, when it came, was ludicrous considering my reaction.

'Can you identify that as Lesley, Mrs Downey?'

I bit my lip hard and nodded. It was Lesley as I would never wish to remember her, but it was Lesley. It was the final image of her, one which would remain with me for too many years . . . the image of a child in pain and terror. I was vaguely aware of the policeman taking his leave and of Alan going with him into the hall. I lay and wept, wondering at the monsters that had taken the photographs . . . the pathetic parodies of pornography that had so obviously failed. In the photographs there was nothing but terror. Maybe it was the realisation that their depraved attempts to spoil and corrupt had failed to touch the essential innocence of my little girl which had driven them to kill her.

Alan came back into the room, tears streaming down his face.

'Alan ... Alan, he said that they'd selected two photographs that weren't so bad. In God's name what are the others like?'

He shook his head desperately. 'Don't, Ann. Don't think about them.'

But I did think about them. I still think about them. I think about them when people who should know better try to get parole for the beasts who tortured, humiliated and killed my daughter. I remember the look of dread in Lesley's eyes as she posed under the crazed commands of those sub-human creatures that some would say have paid enough and should be released on to the streets. I think of the tied hands raised in prayer and struggle and imagine Lesley's state of mind as they subjected her to crueller and yet more obscene acts for their camera's probing lens.

They couldn't know what Alan and I knew ... or perhaps they found out and it gave added savour to their planned and calculated monstrosities ... Lesley was the shyest and most modest girl alive. PE at school was a nightmare to her. She hated to do handstands, in case her knickers showed. At bathtime the bathroom door was firmly locked; her innate modesty would not allow her to be seen undressing or in the bath by her brothers.

They would tease her about her shyness, and especially about a photograph of her taken at the seaside when she was a toddler. It showed her standing at the edge of the sea with bucket and spade in hand, her dress tucked into her knickers. The innocence of that scene and the cruel attempt at pornographic humiliation I had just witnessed were in stark and terrible contrast. I tried to imagine what it must have been like for Lesley having to undress while two weird strangers stood by sneering and laughing. It is impossible to imagine. In 25 years I have never been able to feel what she must have felt. Maybe my inability is a protection from the madness that would surely follow if I were to have to undergo, even mentally, what she had to.

'Oh Alan, thank God. There can be nothing worse than that!' But of course there was. There was somthing infinitely worse. But first there was the night to get through.

I don't know which was more painful . . . lying in the curtained darkness struggling in vain to drive the images of Lesley away or slipping into bouts of drug-induced sleep where subconscious scenes from Hell supplied the details of the photographs I had not seen. Awake, I was tortured by the memory of Lesley lying on the cold slab of the mortuary. Hands were constantly pulling me back from contact with her ruined body. The green sheet and what it hid taunted with its discreet horrors. I thrashed around in the confines of the bed and prayed for the pills to take me away from such grotesque reality. When I slipped for brief periods into unconsciousness the photographs came alive. Lesley was abused, humiliated and degraded before my eyes and I screamed helplessly while it went on and on. I would awaken, sweating in horror, then reality took over again. That night I knew that Hell was real. Hell was here and now . . . and I was in it.

But Hell is subtle and just when you think that there is an infinitesimal chance of coming to terms with your agony it presents you with something worse, something so awful that it lies beyond any conceivable scale of terror.

It started the next morning. I saw my reflection for a moment in the window of the police car that was speeding Alan and me to Hyde police station. The double dose of Valium had made me curiously apathetic. I remember looking at my reflection and thinking 'That woman's very ill – that woman's me.' Alan was holding my hand tightly but I was aware only distantly of this. We swept through the streets and I recall gazing at the people and the shops and the world out there going about its routine business. I reflected dully and as a matter of unresented fact that I would never be part of that world again. I had been separated from blessed normality and would never walk its pavements again. I became aware of Alan's hand and through the Valium haze sensed dimly that he was cut off from normality as well. The drug was cruel and did not allow me to express my gratitude or even realise what he was going through.

'I'm sorry, sir.'

We were in the police station and yet again Alan was

being separated from me when I needed him most. I now realise how much worse it was for him; after all, he knew what it was that awaited me in the CID office into which I was ushered. I went without resentment or fear; the drugs had temporarily suppressed my seething emotions. I was moving like a zombie.

In front of me was a desk and a chair facing the desk. A man was coming round the desk and taking my hand. A man was talking to me.

'Superintendent Bob Talbot, Mrs Downey. It was good of you to come.'

I wasn't aware that there had been a choice. There probably hadn't been. Our lives seemed to be in other people's hands now . . . much as Lesley's had been. Bob Talbot indicated the chair and the officer who had brought me in pulled it back for me to sit. I was vaguely aware of him remaining very close at my shoulder, possibly to support me if I passed out.

I tried to focus my eyes. The wooden top of the desk was clear . . . except fot a tape-recorder. It meant nothing to me. Alan had done his best to protect me from the details that were starting to emerge in the press and which he had picked up in conversations with the police. He had done his job too well. The significance of the tape-recorder was totally lost on me.

'A tape has been found, Ann. It is not pleasant but I must ask you if you can identify Lesley's voice. I have a daughter of my own so I know how you must be feeling.'

'Oh no you don't,' I thought. 'You mean well but you haven't a clue how I'm feeling. Nobody has.'

'I'm going to turn this on and then ask you if you recognise the voice, OK?'

I must have nodded because I saw his hand move towards the switch and the reels begin to turn. My eyes were riveted on the smoothness of the silently turning tape. Adrenalin had flushed the Valium out of my system and I was fully alert. I was going to hear my Lesley's voice. After all the months I would hear the voice I had longed for. In my wild expectation I had forgotten the warning he had given me: 'It is not pleasant.'

The tape fed silently across the empty spool. There was a static hiss but still nothing. Then suddenly there was music . . . music increasing in volume . . . the insistent, stupid music of 'The Little Drummer Boy' . . . music increasing in volume . . . and then a voice – a voice harsh and cruel.

'What is your name?'

The music monotonously drummed on for a few seconds and then: 'Lesley . . . Lesley Ann.'

There was bewilderment and terror in her voice.

'What's your name?'

This time the question was shouted. It was the bullying shout of an interrogator.

'Lesley Ann Weston.'

Her voice was trembling. It was a voice struggling through tears. She had even got the surname she had happily accepted wrong in her horrified confusion. The mad, monotonous music rattled on. The pauses were terrifying as it was impossible to avoid imagining what was being done to the small victim in between spoken demands and pleas.

'Please don't make me take my clothes off.'

The voice was very small and desperate.

'Please don't make me get undressed again. Let me go home to Mummy.'

'Shut your mouth! If you don't shut your mouth and stop crying I'll give you another good hiding.'

The voice, low and venomous, was that of a woman. It was obscene.

'I won't tell nobody what you've done to me. Just let me go home to Mummy. She'll be so angry with me for not going right home. Let me go. I won't tell anyone, honest.'

A hand was reaching forward. The tape was quickly switched off. I was numb. This wasn't happening. This was part of the nightmare. I would wake up soon and everything would be as it was . . . everything would be as it was.

'Was that Lesley?'

His voice was choked. I looked up. There were tears in his eyes. So many tears . . . so many questions.

I tried to speak, but my whole body had tensed. I was in some sort of muscular spasm. My mouth and throat were dry. I couldn't even croak. I swallowed hard and heard my voice as from a distance.

'You know it was. Why did you make me listen to it? Why couldn't you leave me alone?'

I could hear my voice rising. I was slipping out of

control again. The muscular paralysis was going and I started to shake uncontrollably.

'I'm so sorry. So deeply sorry. We had to do it.'

Bob Talbot's voice sounded ashamed. He was a good man trapped by regulations and procedure. Trapped . . . but not as Lesley had been, my little Lesley trapped by monsters and pleading for mercy forever on electronic tape.

'We wouldn't have made you go through it if there was any other way.'

He was genuine. He meant it. I couldn't hate him for what he had to do. I had hate for nobody . . . for nobody but that other voice on the tape. He had switched it off but still it ran. It's still running a quarter of a century later.

Seven photographs and I had seen only two. Seventeen minutes of tape and I had heard only a minute or less. What unimaginable monstrosities remain hidden from me? They do not remain unimagined. Through the sleeping tablets and the tranquillisers the images insist on smearing themselves across my brain. Maybe the imagined horrors are worse than Lesley had to suffer . . . but what if they are not? What if Brady and Hindley's sick imaginations dreamed up more than I could to fuel their foul, deadly games?

His hand had reached into my field of vision and switched the tape off, but the tape is still running. Every day and every night it runs. Every day and every night I hear those contradictory voices. The voice of she whom

91

in this world I probably loved the most . . . my Lesley.
The voice of she whom in this world and the next I will
pursue for vengeance . . . Myra Hindley.

11

Monday, 25 October 1965 – the day before Lesley Ann's funeral. I don't think that either Alan or I could have coped with the details involved in arranging the funeral. The death of a child is harrowing enough but the circumstances of Lesley's tragic end made such practicalities impossible to undertake. Fortunately the arrangements were taken out of our hands by those good, kind people of Charnley Walk and Miles Platting. The £100 that they had collected for the reward was used to pay for the bulk of the funeral costs and they took over the organisation for us as well. I don't know what we would have done if it had not been for them.

We were not allowed to have Lesley's coffin in the house overnight. I don't know why we were denied permission for the sad remains of our little girl to share a last night under our roof. Perhaps it was the undertakers; perhaps the police. It was another example of the system . . . the system that seemed to remove us ever further from the normal rituals of grief. Instead we spent Monday in a state of distraction. Now I think it might have been for the best. At the time the constant ringing of the doorbell and the delivery of wreaths and floral tributes seemed exhausting. It *was* exhausting, but it was a distraction. Before the twilight fell on that grey October day we had been forced to start putting wreaths in the bedrooms. I remember that by the morning of the funeral the wreaths from relatives, friends and total strangers spread across our front garden and into the gardens of neighbours on both sides.

Fortunately my sister Elsie and her husband John were spending the night with us together with our friends the Keatings from Middleton. Again the distraction of having others with us was beneficial, otherwise I think our hearts would have broken with the grief of Lesley's imminent departure. We read the cards on the wreaths, drank endless cups of coffee and noticed rather warily the army of photographers gathering outside the close in Bunkers Hill Road. A uniformed policeman had been posted at the door and more police prevented the media from encroaching closer. At least we were to be spared the indignities of ten months previously when Charnley Walk swarmed with oafish maniacs waving microphones and cameras.

We all deal with grief in different ways. There is no set rule or pattern for how the human mind and heart struggle to cope with the burden of death. I think I understood Alan's sudden impulse to start painting the exposed strip of floorboard at the edges of the carpet on the stairs. He was probably trying to bring some neatness and order into lives which were falling apart. Here was something that he could see through to completion; something that would have a beginning, a middle and an end. So much in our lives had become fractured, uncertain, incomplete. It was while he was doing this that a very strange incident occurred.

I had asked him to leave the front door ajar as the smell of paint got on my chest. I was standing in the living-room doorway telling Alan about a wreath that had been sent by the Trinity Church choir when the front door was suddenly pushed wide open. Alan and I stared in silent astonishment as two huge white dogs came quietly but determinedly into the hallway. They looked at each of us and then, without any sound or show of further interest, walked calmly through the house and out through the back kitchen door. We looked at each other in bewilderment. We had not imagined it, for they could both be seen walking together across the open land behind the house. Alan went out into the garden and watched them heading steadily and quietly towards the moors beyond. To this day neither Alan nor I can fathom what those dogs came for or what, if anything, they signified. A few days later Alan went round the neighbours asking who owned those two very large dogs. Nobody had ever seen them or had any knowledge of them. He even enquired of farmers on the moor's edge, but nobody knew of any farmer with dogs of such a description.

Tuesday dawned cold and grey but dry. I saw the dawn break as I had not caught a wink of sleep. Despite the usual dose of Tuinal and Diazepam sleep had evaded me. I think I was the first up, making coffee to try to drive the muzziness of the drugs from my head. This was a big day. It was Lesley's day. I must not let her down. Soon Alan and the boys were with me. We stood in the kitchen and smiled sadly at each other. No matter what happened for the rest of that day, no matter what had happened to us in the past year, we were still together. We had survived and would go on surviving. I turned and looked through the window to hide my sudden tears. My girl was missing . . . my little Lesley Ann. But I turned back to my men. It was Lesley that this day was all about.

The hours until the hearse and the cars making up the cortege arrived at 10 a.m. drifted by in quiet talk and the arrival of yet more floral tributes. Friends and neighbours from both Charnley Walk and Hattersley dropped in with words of quiet support and condolence. Terry Downey, Lesley's father, arrived together with his brothers Patrick, Jimmy and Gerald. We were vaguely aware of crowds gathering in the streets of the estate as visitors commented on how difficult it had been to get through. I hoped that the solemnity of the occasion was not going to be spoiled. My Lesley deserved the best.

Tommy and Brett were hugging me before being taken to a friend's house for the day. Alan and I didn't feel that they were up to coping with such a long and distressing day as lay ahead.

'She's here,' said somebody who had been watching for the hearse from the front window. We watched the long, black vehicles manoeuvring in the confines of the Close. Lesley had come home at last. I noticed the wreaths that by now covered not only our garden but seemed to spread right along the gardens of our block. On that cold, grey day the autumn gardens seemed to have burst into miraculous colour for the long-awaited return of our little girl.

It wasn't until we had left Bowden Close and were slowly driving through the streets of Hattersley that the extent of people's love for Lesley really struck us. The crowds lining the roads were huge. A journey to Trinity Church in Miles Platting that normally took about fifteen minutes in a car took us over an hour. A police car and motorcycle escort cleared the route and made sure that every junction was clear for us, but still crowds pressed forward in silent tribute. Alan pressed my hand and we drove slowly on, aware that there was good in the world – aware that the evil our Lesley had experienced was a sick and sorry deviation from the norm.

Finally we were in Miles Platting and struggling through crowds that were even more vast. Trinity Church, where Lesley had gone to Sunday School and sung in the choir, was under siege. I think that through my tears and when not blinded by the flash of cameras I recognised kind faces from our days here. I had no time to acknowledge them, for Lesley's coffin was being carried slowly up the steps of the church of which she had been so much a part. And then that kind, generous man Harold Ford was at my side. The Reverend Ford had helped us in so many ways and now he helped me at yet another crisis. His arm supported me strongly, he whispered words of encouragement and helped me down the aisle of the crowded church, following the little coffin in which my daughter lay.

I will never forget the quiet words which began the service.

'One of our flock is not with us today . . .'

My eyes went to the space in the choir where Lesley normally sat. A space had been left and the emptiness said everything. The service was a gentle and loving farewell from a church and community that had taken Lesley to its heart in the few months we had lived in the district. My eyes were full of tears throughout the service, like those of any mother who had come to bury her child, but when the Reverend Ford announced the 23rd Psalm I broke into racking sobs of pain. It had been Lesley's favourite and she had never seemed so close as at that moment. The words drifted in and out of my consciousness. They seemed so terribly apt, so harrowingly relevant.

'He maketh me to lie down in green pastures . . . He guideth me in paths of righteousness . . . even though I walk through the valley of the shadow of death . . . I will fear no evil . . . You prepare a table for me in the presence of my enemies . . . and I will dwell in the house of the Lord forever . . .'

There was a loud Amen that seemed to echo strangely. I looked to Alan in puzzlement.

'There are speakers outside,' he whispered. 'There are still hundreds who can't get in.'

I nodded. So much love . . . it seemed to break in waves throughout the church. So much love, yet Lesley had met with beasts who didn't know the meaning of the word, who knew only the sick lust of their warped appetites. I looked up and my blurred vision took in the coffin, Alan sitting close by my side and the kind, concerned face of Harold Ford.

'He leadeth me beside quiet waters . . . He restoreth my soul.' The crowds again – silent crowds watching the coffin being placed carefully once more within the flower-filled hearse – Harold Ford riding with Lesley as we followed through the silent, crowded streets. Another four or five miles to Southern Cemetery – the same police escort – the same sad, curious faces watching Lesley's little coffin travelling its last journey. Police at the junctions again trying to ease our progress through the cold, grey afternoon. At last Princess Parkway, where the crowds were even denser; a right-hand turn and the gates of the old cemetery, now swarming with press and television crews. A pause while some administrative detail was checked at the lodge house.

Still with the police escort we followed the hearse as it slowly progressed through the tall, dark memorials of the old Victorian section of the cemetery. Angels of dirty stone looked down on marble slabs that hid the source of some older grief. I followed where mothers themselves long dead must have wept for children and other loved ones in days long past. Today it was Lesley's turn to be wept over. Weeping there was in plenty. We crossed Nell Lane into the newer section of Southern Cemetery.

A discreet police cordon kept back the hundreds who came silently to the graveside. I felt cold and empty. Alan hovered nervously at my side, ready to hold me or support me. Terry gripped my hand tightly. He was trying so hard to be grown-up, but this was his first experience of death and its rituals. His drawn, serious face stared in awe at the hillocks of flowers and wreaths that had come to welcome Lesley to her final resting-place. He pointed out our cross of roses at the head of the grave. I nodded and tried to smile through my misery.

'Our Father which art in Heaven . . .'

The Reverend Ford's voice quavered for a moment. This quiet, kind man, so accustomed to officiating at sad occasions, was moved despite his experience. What hope was there for me? The prayer ended. The coffin was lowered gently into the cold, black earth. I stood, trembling with an agony of loneliness as my daughter, my Lesley, was taken from me forever. Alan was supporting me and whispering to me.

'You've done marvellously, darling. A handful of earth . . .'

I looked puzzled for a moment and then I understood.

As Alan held my arm I stooped and took a handful of damp soil from beside the grave and threw it down on to the coffin. It was a terrible sound, a sound of utter finality. It was a door closing forever. I felt myself buckling at the knees; I heard a low moan and then Harold Ford was at my side.

'Come on, Ann. You've coped marvellously. I think you should rest in the car for a moment.'

And so he led me back to the waiting cars. I turned and saw Alan looking down into the grave. Family and close friends were pressing round him. I turned away and staggered with the help of Reverend Ford to the shelter of the car. I wasn't aware of it at the time but television cameras and press were quietly recording every moment of our misery. This time they were restrained. The media's usual brash, intrusive style was abandoned. Even the hardened press corps sensed something special about that cold autumn day.

For half an hour I huddled in the back of the car while well-wishers, most of them strangers, came to offer their hands and silent sympathy. People I had never seen before in my life came to wish us well, offer condolences and share my tears. It was as if they felt more had been lost than a child by its mother. The world had lost Lesley and what she represented: quiet innocence, gentle trust, childlike love.

The police suggested to Alan a different route back to Hattersley as the crowds at the main gate were too great to penetrate. Finally together again, we left the cemetery by a side road and took the long road home. I didn't notice the crowds still lining the roads. I huddled in a corner of the back seat and wept for my loss. It was one of the few times when even Alan could not get through to me. I was a mother alone, supporting a weight of misery that only a mother can know.

I think there was some sort of tea at home prepared by a couple of the neighbours. People said things and hands were held. I recall Harold Ford's quiet strength and gentle words of comfort and support; and Alan, doing his best to calm Terry, who was devastated by the whole day. Thank God Tommy and Brett were staying at the home of some friends. I would have been incapable of offering them the comfort due from a mother. And then they were all gone.

We collapsed on the sofa after Alan had turned on the television to distract us. We were not watching it. It was simply a noise in the silence that allowed us to concentrate on our individual misery. I had taken my pills on Alan's instructions. I think I remember hearing the voice of a news announcer describing the funeral and mentioning that the district had 'never seen such a vast number of people'. I drifted off, thinking to myself that there was still goodness in the world. I drifted deeper into a drugged haze and heard a small voice crying somewhere. It was Lesley's voice, shrill and frightened.

'Please let me go back to my mother . . .'

We had buried Lesley, but not the memories that are forever associated with her, memories that remain very precious and tender and good ... but indelibly stained by the evil slime of the creatures that took her away from us.

12

Over the years the public has come to know me for my strong opposition to those misguided public figures who advocate the release, through the parole system, of convicted murderers serving life sentences. How could any mother who has lost a child to a cold-blooded killer have any other view on this issue? The life sentence of grief that I am serving makes my opposition to the freeing of killers absolute and unyielding.

If you had listened, as I did, to a tape-recording of two grown people cold-bloodedly and systematically abusing, torturing and finally killing your child, you too would move heaven and earth to ensure they never breathed free air again. Ian Brady has at least had the good sense to insist over the years that he does not wish ever to leave prison, maybe because of the shame in his unfathomable heart, maybe through fear of the death he would inevitably suffer at the hands of those who would ensure that his freedom was short-lived. Whatever the reason, he is behind bars and seems set to remain in that condition. The grotesque, almost unbelievable fact, is that Brady's perverted partner in crime – Myra Hindley – is supported in her desire to walk free on parole. She is backed by a strange and motley crew of prostitutes, journalists, criminals and even a peer of the realm, Lord Longford.

Ever since the trial of those two monsters at Chester Assizes in April of 1966 and the revelations of their secret reign of terror I have been determined to fight for justice, thus ensuring that a life sentence for such vermin is exactly what it says: *life*.

My campaign has been costly, not just in money terms, but in terms of health and personal reputation. My obsession with keeping Hindley and others of her species behind bars has brought me into friendship with but also opposition to some notable personalities. Some may consider me a crank; others may feel I am a spokesperson for their own unvoiced beliefs: it doesn't matter. So long as I can do my utmost to ensure killers and sadists never walk free or have the opportunity to kill again I will consider the cost worthwhile.

It was less than two years after the doors shut on Brady and Hindley that I became publicly active in my opposition to the 'soft' approach. In the 1966 General Election my brother-in-law Patrick Downey stood as an Independent candidate in the Nelson and Colne constituency in North East Lancashire. This was the seat of Sidney Silverman, the Labour MP who had guided his 'no hanging' bill through Parliament and on to the statute books. I suppose my resolve was focused on this man in particular, for otherwise Brady and Hindley would surely have paid on the gallows for their sins. Patrick Downey's political platform was based almost entirely on his opposition to the abolition of hanging for crimes of the kind committed by the killers of his niece.

Alan and I toured the constituency with Patrick Downey in a car equipped with loudspeakers, declaiming our message to the voters of Nelson and Colne. A memorable confrontation for those who were there on the streets occurred one day when we accidentally found ourselves at the same junction as Sidney Silverman in his campaign car. That amplified exchange of views was somewhat frank and to the point, to put it mildly. At least I got a lot of my frustration and rage at such 'do-gooders' off my chest.

A sad and telling footnote to Patrick Downey's ill-fated campaign came after the results were announced. It was clear that Patrick was taking his arguments into unsympathetic territory and in the event he lost his deposit. Patrick coped with the disappointment, but the young man who had acted as his political agent was so distraught at the rejection of our arguments that he committed suicide, by hanging himself, not many months later. Maybe in some macabre way the evil influence of Brady and Hindley was still reaching out from behind the bars and steel doors that kept them off the streets.

Many years later I was on Robert Kilroy-Silk's morning television programme which was debating capital punishment and met Albert Pierrepoint, who had been the public executioner. At first I did not know who he was, but was fascinated by this old man who wore a black glove on his left hand. Somebody explained to me who he was and the symbolic covering of the hand that pulled the trap on those who rejected the laws of society. The programme turned out to be quite lively, which is not surprising given the importance of the issue under discussion. It was later at the hotel arranged by the producer for our accommodation that I had private words with Mr Pierrepoint. He was a very quiet and undemonstrative man who was clearly used to the curiosity of the public in what had been a unique occupation. We sat and had a drink in the bar, talking about Lesley and the whole business of capital punishment as a deterrent and as a fitting punishment for certain crimes.

Suddenly this unassuming and controlled man turned to me and with considerable fervour said, 'Ann, if it were possible I would come out of retirement tomorrow and hang those two buggers for nothing.'

I nodded. I understood his loathing of the monsters. At that moment I wished that Pierrepoint, who had hung Ruth Ellis, the last woman to receive capital punishment in Britain, could hang just one more woman. If this sounds vindictive, try to remember what I heard on that tape, try to remember what that so-called woman did to my child.

The person with whom over the years I have had most consistent contact concerning the issue of parole for life-sentence prisoners, and its denial for Hindley in particular, is Lord Longford. I find him a most dangerous and woolly-minded buffoon whose views are taken seriously because of his accidental social status rather than because of the validity of his ideas. He has come to represent for me the face of confusion – the dangerous confusion that could lead to the release of murderers like Myra Hindley into a world where innocent children still walk unaware of the abuses being planned in the warped minds of certain adults.

It was in about 1969 that I went down to London with Eric Towner of the *Manchester Evening News* to beg Longford to stop his campaign for Brady and Hindley to be considered for parole. There was no talking to the man. He sat smugly behind his desk in the offices of the publishers Sidgwick & Jackson, of which he was chairman, and listened with deaf ears to my pleas. He hasn't a clue of the struggle for decency and survival that goes on day by day where ordinary people dwell. It is like trying to talk to a fossil.

After a while he stopped the conversation and asked me if I would like to 'take wine' with him or have 'a spot of lunch'. I told him that it would choke me. In a vague and distracted way he seemed surprised. He left the room for a while to speak to Eric Towner, leaving me alone. Lord Longford's secretary bustled in and proceeded to tell me in detail about Myra Hindley and how Longford had found her a changed woman, how she had become a good Christian and how she was studying hard for qualifications. Lord Longford and his secretary clearly spent a lot of time out of the office mixing with the filth of society.

The noble lord returned and there was a little more discussion in which theoretical Christianity seemed to be the main prop of his argument and the facts of the streets the basis of mine. It was clearly no good talking to this blinkered dinosaur.

I concluded by telling him quite clearly, 'Lord Longford, I will fight you every inch of the way. You will not succeed in your crazy plans.'

Fortunately some years had passed before I found myself in Lord Longford's company again. It was 1977; the whole issue of parole was topical once again since it was now ten years since the Brady/Hindley sentence had begun. Such was the furore in the press that the *Brass Tacks* programme devoted itself to a debate. A phone-in formed part of the programme, together with a discussion by people directly or indirectly concerned with the issue of parole for life detainers. The opponents of such parole, apart from myself, were Wyn Pilkington, now working with the Murder Victims' Association, Joan Yonkers and Charles Oxley of the Victims of Law and Order and Arthur Benfield representing the police.

Lord Longford appeared on the programme to defend his campaign, together with a rather bizarre collection of supporters. These included Sarah Trevelyan, daughter of Lord Trevelyan, for many years the British film censor. This young lady had made something of a name for herself at the time by marrying the notorious murderer Jimmy Boyle, whom she had met on prison visits. In addition there was a journalist from the *Manchester Evening News* as well as Myra Hindley's sister, Maureen Smith, wife of Dave Smith who had been heavily involved with Brady and Hindley. If one is known by the company one keeps then Lord Longford was making quite a name for himself. Janie Jones, the 'vice queen', made up his team.

The argument flowed back and forth, and I believe our side acquitted itself well. In the phone-in Lord Longford displayed an apparent inability to handle callers who held a different opinion from his own. Longford's case rests mainly on his vague assurances that Myra Hindley is a changed woman. I find this a very strange argument. The mental state of a person is very difficult to define or judge, and if one is to be able to claim with any authority that someone has 'changed' this presupposes that one knew her as she was. One of the calls to Lord Longford was from an ex-nun who had visited Hindley in gaol. She was explaining that she had found Hindley to be a very dangerous, untrustworthy woman. Lord Longford put the phone down as the caller was still speaking with the comment that if he had known he was talking to an *ex*-nun he would never have picked up the phone in the first place.

Many of the newspapers the next day made much of the fact that another caller during the *Brass Tacks* phone-in was the father of John Kilbride, another of Hindley and Brady's victims. Lord Longford's team did not seem to take seriously the grief-stricken father's promise on air, 'I will kill Myra Hindley if she ever gets out!'

Lord Longford probably does not realise how many others share Mr Kilbride's views. Once freed, Myra Hindley would not last a couple of days, wherever in the world she tried to hide. There is still such a thing as natural justice.

Such was the strength of feeling, even ten years after the trial, that Hindley's sister had to be filmed in silhouette for the programme. She felt her own life to be in danger, not just because of the blood relationship with her perverted sister but because of a lingering public feeling that her husband Dave Smith's involvement with Brady and Hindley was deeper than had emerged at the trial.

After the programme was over Maureen Smith was hustled out under escort while others went up to 'hospitality' to relax or continue the debate. Lord Longford and Janie Jones continued to assure me what a model prisoner Hindley had become. Janie Jones, who had talked with Hindley when they were in Holloway together, gave her prison 'chum' a glowing reference. It struck me later that a woman whose word wouldn't be taken seriously if she offered a reference for a toilet-cleaner was being granted credence by Lord Longford for a matter as grave as this: whether or not to release a cold-blooded child-killer and multiple murderer. She and the noble lord assured me that Hindley would like me to visit her in pirson. I assured them both that I could not forgive such a monster just because she claimed to be 'sorry'.

'God will never forgive you, Mrs West, or even Lesley. You see, you can't be a Christian while still wanting revenge.'

I thanked the patronising peer for his religious instruction and said, 'I don't want revenge, I want justice!'

I'm not sure he really understood that I knew the difference. I wonder if he knows it himself.

One remark made on camera by Maureen Smith on the *Brass Tacks* programme must have confused viewers, for it meant nothing except to Alan and myself. In response to a remark I had made about never forgetting what had been done to Lesley she turned to me and said, 'You've got a short memory, Mrs West.'

She was referring to an incident in 1966. One afternoon, not long after the trial and subsequent imprisonment of Brady and Hindley, there had been a knock on the door at Bowden Close. I was particularly heavily sedated during that period. Alan answered the door while I lay in a half-doped state on the sofa. A young man standing rather nervously on the step introduced himself as Dave Smith. The name meant nothing to Alan at first. I was dimly aware of the conversation on the doorstep, hearing it in a detached sort of way as if it were a radio play.

'Do you know who I am?'

'I'm afraid not. Should I?'

'I'm Hindley's brother-in-law. I gave evidence against the two of them at the trial.'

This didn't have much significance to me in my prevailing mental state. The pills were too powerful to allow me to react. I was aware of Alan asking him in and I briefly looked up as the tall, rather hesitant young man came in and sat down. I drifted in and out of consciousness. I heard Terry's voice and smiled at him as he entered the room.

'Isn't he like Lesley!' exclaimed Dave Smith.

Something was wrong. My brain struggled against the chains that were holding it from involvement in the conversation. Something was very wrong. I knew that Terry and Lesley bore a strong resemblance but it was not one that came out in photographs. How did this young man know if he had only seen photographs in the press or on our 'wanted' poster? Suddenly a flow of adrenalin cleared the effects of the drugs. I feigned sleepiness but listened very carefully to the tale that he told.

Some of the things he revealed we knew about already. The police had given us certain facts and we had picked up pieces of information from the press and the trial itself. But there were other things that had never come out before and which had never, to our knowledge, been spoken of before. Some of the details he told us were significantly different from the story that was told at the trial.

I listened in silent revulsion as he told of Myra Hindley coming round to the flat he lived in with Maureen Smith at Underwood Close on the Hattersley estate. She had apparently turned up late at night to ask him to bring a pram round to the house she was sharing with Brady a few streets away. For some reason he went with her to the house on Wardle Brook Avenue but without the pram. Once outside Hindley had asked him to wait until she called him. Some moments passed and then he was signalled in. According to Dave Smith he found Myra Hindley in the front room, semi-naked, flaunting herself before 17-year-old Edward Evans who was sitting on a sofa. Behind Evans was Ian Brady with an axe raised. Then began an orgy of violence in which Edward Evans was hacked again and again around the head and shoulders.

I couldn't believe what I was hearing. Why was this shy, stuttering young man telling us all this? He continued to tell of Brady finishing off Edward Evans by throttling him with a cord until the gurgling screams ceased.

'This is the messiest one yet,' gloated Myra Hindley, according to her brother-in-law. There was not the slightest show of remorse, more a sadistic glee at the terrible bloodbath in which all three of them stood. Smith went on to tell us of cleaning up the mess and the wrapping up of Evans's body in a carpet. Grotesque as all this was, my mind would not let me forget those apparently casual words of his: 'Isn't he like Lesley?'

Still he went on, telling us stories of his times with Brady and of his weird friend's erratic temper and vile sense of 'humour'. We became increasingly puzzled as to why this young man had come to us, of all people, to tell his sick tales. I heard him telling Alan of an occasion

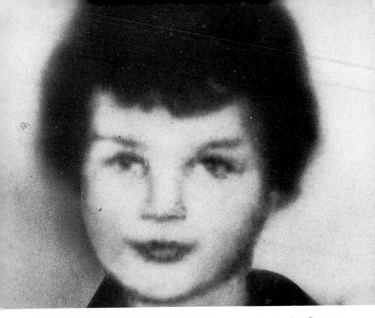

Above: Lesley Ann Downey, wearing the coat she wore on Boxing Day 1964, photographed a week before her death.

Left: Lesley with two of her brothers, Tommy and Brett, 1964.

Left: Myra Hindley and
Ian Brady (below),
sentenced in 1966 to life
imprisonment for the
Moors Murders.

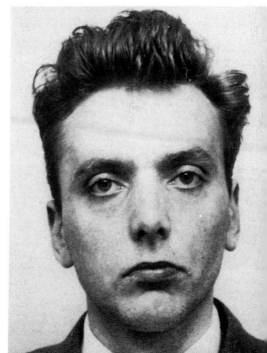

Left: Ann and
Lesley, June 1964.

IN LOVING MEMORY OF
OUR DARLING
LESLEY ANN
BELOVED DAUGHTER OF
ANN AND TERRY DOWNEY
DIED 26TH DEC. 1964 AGED 10.
A TINY FLOWER LENT NOT GIVEN
TO BUD ON EARTH AND BLOOM

Silent, mourning crowds on the day of Lesley's funeral.

Above right: Ann and Alan West outside Hindley's prison in June 1987.

Above left: Brady: in 1987 he claimed that he knew of five further bodies on the Moors.

Left: Doris Stokes, the spiritualist, convinced, like Ann West, that Lesley could communicate from beyond the grave.

Above: Ann with Lord Longford at his office in 1968. Lord Longford has campaigned vigorously for Hindley to be paroled; just as vigorously Ann opposes him.

Below: Meeting with John Stalker at a Manchester signing session for his book in 1988. Stalker served as a detective sergeant in the Moors Murders case.

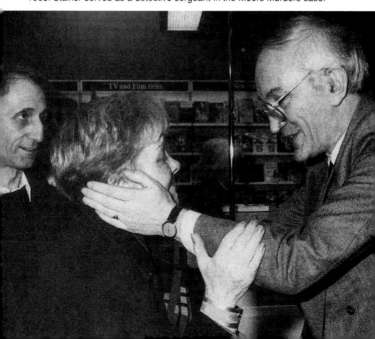

PETITION
CHILDREN IN DANGER

For Child Murder
LIFE MUST MEAN LIFE
TODAY A SO-CALLED "LIFE" SENTENCE IS ONLY 9 YEARS ON AVERAGE

For Child Rape and Child Abuse
SEVERE CUSTODIAL SENTENCES
TODAY IT IS NOT UNUSUAL FOR CHILD RAPISTS AND CHILD MOLESTERS TO BE LET OFF WITH SUSPENDED SENTENCES OR PROBATION

'Let the Punishment Fit the Crime'

Please Support This Petition

MVA

**MURDER
VICTIMS'
ASSOCIATION**

FOUNDER, MRS. ANN WEST, 20 Grindley Avenue, Chorlton, Manchester

when he had been travelling with Hindley and Brady in the mini-van and they were overtaken by a couple in a sports car. Brady had been infuriated and urged Myra to overtake the sports car at all costs. After she had succeeded in doing so, Brady wound down the window and hurled an empty wine bottle at the windscreen of the speeding car, only narrowly missing it. It was quite clear he would have been supremely happy to see the couple killed, even though he hadn't a clue who they were.

My mind was in turmoil. Why was this strange youth telling us of his time with that demented couple – the two creatures we had every reason to loathe most in the world? Why did he mention Terry's similarity to Lesley? Why was he watching us so keenly for our reactions? Dave Smith seemed to sense that we were not in the mood for his macabre revelations and finished by letting us know Ian Brady's favourite joke. Totally sick, it was just what one might expect of a mind capable of devising the foul deeds he perpetrated with his partner on so many children: what, if asked, was the difference between a lorryload of sand and a lorryload of babies? Smith recalled the glee with which Brady would give the answer: 'You can't unload sand with a pitchfork!'

I felt my stomach heaving. Would this never end? I heard Alan explaining diplomatically that I needed some rest and finally Smith was shown the door. Alone at last, we sat and stared at each other. The nightmare of Lesley's disappearance, the discovery of her body, the photographs, the tapes . . . all took on a terrible clarity from listening to the ramblings of Brady's strange friend.

Over the next few days Alan and I found ourselves coming back again and again to that apparently casual remark by Smith about Terry's physical resemblance to Lesley. It began to obsess us. We remembered the claims made by Brady at the trial concerning two men who had brought Lesley to the house on Wardle Brooke Avenue and had also taken her away. Presumably he was lying in order to try to get a lighter sentence. But what if there had been *some* truth in his claim? Had Smith, who had been a party to their slaughter of Edward Evans, been involved in the torture and death of Lesley? By the Saturday after Smith's uninvited visit we were convinced that he was involved in some way. We recalled how Brady and Hindley were reputed to have got some sort of strange thrill from going out of their way to see or find out how the parents of their victims were coping with the loss they had brought about. Was Smith acting as their eyes and ears, even though his friends were locked up? Or was Smith's visit arranged so that he could check on our agony for his own satisfaction?

We were at boiling point by Saturday evening. Without any clear plan other than clearing our hearts of the torment that Smith's visit had increased to an intolerable point, we set out for where he lived with Hindley's sister. Alan remembered that Underwood Close had been mentioned as their address during the trial but other than that we had no more details. We had to ask an elderly gentleman in the street if he knew where the Smiths lived. Maybe he recognised me; perhaps he sensed the fury in our hearts. Whatever the reason, he smiled a smile of satisfaction as he pointed out their flat. Local feeling against the Smiths was running high at that time. If the old gentleman knew what was in our minds he certainly wasn't going to delay us or interfere with our purposes.

Until we stood at the door of the Smiths' flat we didn't know what we wanted. After knocking at the door twice and receiving no reply, despite the lights being on, we were suddenly overcome by rage. Dave Smith had come into our house and our grief without any hindrance; how dare he keep his door closed to us? All at once Alan was kicking furiously at the door. It splintered open at the second kick and we rushed in.

As soon as were inside I realised what I wanted. I had to have a photograph of Maureen's hellish sister. I wanted an original photograph, so that if ever Myra got out I would be able to track her down and give her the punishment she deserved. There was protest and a lot of noise and suddenly I had Maureen Smith's hair in my hands. I struggled with her violently while Alan gave Dave a beating that he would never forget. All our frustration and pent-up outrage was taken out on these kindred of the creatures who had taken Lesley so cruelly from us. I beat Maureen Smith's head against the wall and screamed incoherently at her. I tore at her and for a moment it was as if I had her foul sister in my hands. We were out of control, or perhaps, after all the months of misery and confusion, we were actually *in* control. I remembered that this woman I had by the hair had been reported as saying in some newspaper report, 'They're offering £100 for that kid,' referring to the reward money. I was not supposed to read the reports in case they made me even more upset, but I had read that. Nobody calls my Lesley 'that kid' with anything but affection. There was no affection in Maureen Smith and so I punished her.

We left them. They were in a pretty bad state but I felt no compassion for them. Compassion had been lacking in Lesley's final hours, so they would receive none from me. We went to bed that night having purged ourselves of just a little of our frustration.

The postscript to the incident came the next morning. There was a knock on our door at 8 a.m. which was answered by Alan. A uniformed policeman and policewoman asked if they could come in to discuss some trouble the previous evening. We were asked if we had gone to the Smiths' house and when we admitted that we had the policewoman revealed a plastic bag.

'Apparently there was some trouble?'

We agreed that things had got rather rough. The policewoman held out the plastic bag for my inspection. It contained quite a quantity of black hair.

'Were you intending to make a black wig, Mrs West?'

We were told that at the time there would be no charges but were also warned that if there were any other similar incidents the police would have no choice but to prosecute. There were no more incidents with the Smiths, but to this day I am not convinced that Dave Smith had told anything like the full story of his relationship with Brady and Hindley.

Before I digressed to explain the background to
Maureen Smith's cryptic remark on the *Brass Tacks*
programme I was outlining my long-running struggle
with those who would seriously support parole for
Hindley, Lord Longford in particular. I vividly recall a
daytime television debate chaired by Sarah Kennedy
during which the MP Nicholas Winterton outlined his
views particularly eloquently, to the obvious discomfort
of his opponent from the Upper House. Instead of
attempting to respond with calm and logical arguments
all the peer could manage to do was stutter: 'That's all
crap!' Perhaps the blue-blooded orator had been mixing
for too long with the likes of Janie Jones and Myra
Hindley.

On the same programme, at which I was present in the
studio audience, Longford responded to a member of
the studio audience, who had made a plea that a life
sentence should last a lifetime, with the comment, 'May
God forgive you.'

I was so enraged that I could not help but retort by
saying, 'Myra Hindley is the devil's daughter and you,
Lord Longford, are the devil's disciple!'

It was January 1987 before I had any more direct
contact with this sadly confused old man. I phoned
Longford to ask him what he thought of Myra Hindley
now that she was admitting to two more murders, the
search for the bodies of Keith Bennett and Pauline Reade
on the moors having already made headlines. He told me
that I was eaten away with hate and that I would never
be in good health until I forgave my enemies. He even

went on to refer to Myra Hindley as a 'good Catholic girl'!

Perhaps he sensed my indignation, because he suddenly tried to adopt a friendly tone of voice: 'Can I call you Ann? You can call me Frank.'

I think that perhaps my sarcasm was lost on him when I replied, 'Well, I'm glad that I don't have to call you Lord.'

The conversation concluded with him asking me to come and visit him and have a glass of wine. It was an invitation I found easy to turn down.

13

I have described my grief as a life sentence, which I endure in consequence of what others did to my daughter. I am sure from my contacts with other mothers who have suffered similarly that I am not unique. Life goes on, although there are times when I wish it would cease, and the daily grieving continues unabated.

I made my vow a long time ago that I would not I give up the ghost as long as Hindley lived. Meanwhile Alan and I go on, taking pleasure in our children and grandchildren, living from day to day, hoping that Lesley is at peace at last. But there are bills to be paid and even a modest lifestyle costs money.

In those early days after Lesley's disappearance we were in dire financial straits. Alan's job as a driver for the

Gas Board soon collapsed when he could not turn up for regular duty because of the need to look after me in my heavily sedated condition. He tried other driving jobs, each time refusing to tell the management who he was and how difficult his situation was. Perhaps it was pride; perhaps he didn't want pity; perhaps he wanted to avoid the inevitable curiosity of workmates. None of the firms he briefly worked for knew of his tragic home life, so inevitably he lost the jobs. It was virtually impossible for him to leave me alone in safety as I was either prostrate with grief or under such heavy sedation that I couldn't function properly or with any degree of safety. The days he took off to look after me and Brett would stretch into weeks. Sacking followed sacking. Even after Lesley had been found and laid to rest it continued. I can still recall Alan coming home one day with a strange smile on his face. It was too early for his normal return and I asked him what was up. He told me that he had been given the sack once more, then went on to explain the smile. This was the fifth job in which he had been in trouble with the boss for taking time off to look after me. He was so desperate this time that he had explained who he was and how Lesley's disappearance had affected me. Instead of showing any understanding or compassion the boss had retorted, 'I'm running a business here. I can't be bothered with your petty domestic problems.'

It had clearly satisfied a deep-seated need in Alan to lay out this callous entrepreneur with one blow of his fist. I know from the experience of a quarter of a century what a mild man Alan is. When he heard those words he had struck a blow for natural justice and humanity by laying that hard-hearted businessman out on the floor.

We were on our own. No government funds seemed to exist to help us out in our need. It was years later that we approached the Criminal Injuries Compensation Board. Our application was turned down as Lesley had been discovered over twenty years previously and claims were considered only within a timespan of three years from the discovery of a body. Nobody had told us of the board's existence at the time. It made no difference. We were too late. Bureaucracy allowed not a penny for our misery or loss of earnings. We were the victims of ignorance.

Yet, looking back at those early days after Lesley's death, I have to admit that there were some bright spots in the misery. At times events turned out to be almost comic in a 'black' sort of way. In 1966 Alan thought he had found a way of earning a crust while still having the independence to look after the family and me. A family firm in Hyde ran a fleet of small ice-cream vans that serviced the needs of estates and villages in that particular part of Cheshire and outer Manchester. Since the hours were flexible and it was almost a form of self-employment for Alan it seemed ideal. The Meachie family, who owned the firm, paid the van rental and sold the ice cream to the driver, and the profits were the wage of the particular 'employee'. Alan was taken on. If he didn't sell the ice cream he didn't earn, but there was some sort of security and, more importantly, there was flexibility of hours.

I'm afraid that the attention Alan paid to me and my needs meant that his hours became rather too flexible, even for the generous Meachie family. The van spent more time off the road than on. One afternoon there was a knocking on the door of the house at Bowden Close. It was at a period when we were being particularly harassed by the media. We just couldn't face another interview, so we decided to be 'out'. Alan dragged me behind the sofa and we ducked down like little children playing a game of hide-and-seek. It seemed to have worked as the knocking on the front door ceased. Suddenly there was a tapping at the window behind us. We turned in embarrassment from our hiding-place on the floor. Gazing at us in curiosity from the back garden was Alan's boss from the ice-cream firm!

Once he had come in, Alan explained who we were and our virtual state of siege from the media. Mr Meachie was most understanding. He said that Alan should have told him of our circumstances before. He was incredibly kind, and the three of us laughed at the memory of us crouching behind the sofa under his puzzled gaze. The years have taught me how often comedy and tragedy run in close parallel at times.

But the laughter didn't last long. Our finances were still in a disastrous state, and despite his kindness Mr Meachie was forced to allocate the ice-cream van to someone with more time available. We had endless communications with the National Assistance Board, as it was known in those days. Finally, in sheer frustration, we set off with Brett to the local headquarters in

Glossop. We were at crisis point; it costs a fair amount of money to keep a growing family of boys in a reasonable state, and Brett was in dire need of a new pair of shoes as well. The NAB had written us a whole series of letters in polite bureaucratic jargon explaining that for reasons A, B or C, X, Y or Z we were ineligible for any money.

After a prolonged but fruitless discussion with a number of assistants we reached breaking-point. Every plea we made was met with a stone-wall defence, based on some regulation or other with which we did not, apparently, comply. We were incensed. How much was it costing per week to keep Brady and Hindley in the comfort of their gaols? We, the victims of their casual lust for slaughter, had received nothing.

On impulse we lifted little Brett, now six, on to the counter and told the board officials that as we could not afford to look after him properly they could do the job instead. I felt terrible as we walked away and heard his cries of distress and confusion. There were protests from the counter staff and general astonishment. It was a desperate bluff, a game that we were forced by circumstance to play. We hated every moment of it. Fortunately we had gambled correctly. Before we reached the street doors one of the 'superiors' had stopped us and decided that to ease our current situation he would authorise a one-off payment of £7. Sobbing with distress that we should have come to this, I gathered Brett into my arms and we left for home. I determined from that point onwards that, no matter what, we would try to be independent of those whose lack of imagination or care deprived of us the means to survive. We had taken the worst that chance could throw at us; we would go on fighting on our own.

But sometimes you need help in the fight. The financial struggle was one that we could survive together, but the efforts to cope with Lesley's absence were destroying me. I was taking Valium and sleeping tablets in stronger and stronger doses. Life was fast becoming intolerable. I realised in the intervals between drugged dementia and conscious depression that the family was in despair at my state. In the early 1980s I had mentioned to Alwyn Thomas of *The People* that I would dearly love to try to make some sort of contact with Lesley via Doris Stokes, the well-known medium. *The People* readily agreed to arrange such a session.

With Alan and a reporter and photographer from the newspaper, I went with some trepidation to see Doris. She was a kind and gentle lady in her late seventies. I had been dubious on the journey down to London but as we arrived at her house I became suddenly excited. Perhaps after all the empty years I would somehow be reunited with Lesley at last. I didn't know what to expect. I only knew that my need to speak to Lesley or hear her voice was absolutely overwhelming. The doorbell was answered and impulsively I rushed to Doris Stokes and hugged her. This was the woman who was going to bring Lesley closer to me somehow. I had to show her the affection that Lesley's enforced absence had bottled up for too many years.

Doris Stokes had a kind face but her eyes were dark-ringed, as if acting as a voice for the hundreds of departed souls who spoke through her had taken its toll. A tape-recorder was set up by the reporter but Doris warned me before she began that she could not promise anything. I nodded. I felt so close to Lesley in the presence of this kind old lady that I was on the verge of tears.

It was difficult at first to get the hang of what was happening. Sometimes Doris was speaking to me directly, sometimes she was telling me what Lesley was saying and at other times she spoke directly the words that Lesley was speaking through her. Soon I began to understand the method and found myself moved, quite naturally, by the contact that had at last been made. Listening to the tape later I was particularly impressed by the detail that Doris provided and the way names and places that I had sometimes forgotten came back under Lesley's guidance and insistence. The following are the actual words that Lesley spoke to Doris and myself during that moving and heart-rending morning.

Alan, you're very good to Mum . . . Bill's this side. [*Bill was my father.*] Don't upset yourself about what you read in the papers, Mum, about Myra being paroled. It's not going to happen. That woman will never reform . . . she's just play-acting . . . She's bad, Doris . . . very bad. We were going for some fish and chips. Two of us went with them to show them where the chip shop was . . . We never went home again. Thank you for the red rose by the

127

picture, Mum . . . thank you for that. Alan thinks about me as much as my mum, you know. Edward wants to say hello because no one ever talks to him [*presumably Edward Evans*]. I'm ever so glad you came, Mum, because I wanted to tell you everything is all right now. I spend my time among the children, Mum – the children and the babies who have been taken back because no one wants them. I love them and spend all my time with them. I never had the chance to have babies of my own but I have lots of them to love here . . . Bill's here, Mum . . . and Jim [*my uncle*] wants to say hello . . . and Joe and Philip are here too (*two old friends who were brothers and who died within a couple of years of each other*].

I have fulfilled my life, Mum, but it is a tragedy about John. He shouldn't have come over the way he did. [*John was my nephew. He died three years after Lesley during a simple operation. He and Lesley were great friends.*]

I met a man here called Frank . . . he used to be a policeman at Mill Street . . . He helped when it happened to me . . . and he is over here now. He said he wished they had been able to avoid it happening to me . . . but they did try, Mum.

I see my mum a lot, Doris. They were talking about Spain and I was there. I was listening and I was trying to tell them to go . . . to do it . . . life's too short . . . look how short mine was. [*Two nights previously we had been discussing whether we could afford a package holiday in Spain. We had not discussed it with anyone else.*] Wales was the best holiday I ever had . . . I did have a good time . . . then this happened. I trusted too much. [*A few months before Lesley died she had spent a week in North*

Wales with the Sunday school.]

Don't worry, Alan. Everything will work out. I can see it all from this side. Live your life, Mum. Be happy and do the things you want to do. I'm OK. I'm happy. I know you were afraid that I was on my own . . . but I'm not. Nothing hurts spirit children. We're innocent, so we're loved here and taken care of.

I used to play with Claire all the time, Doris. If I had been playing with Claire when it happened I would not be here now. Muriel too . . . I liked Muriel especially. [*Muriel was a Sunday School teacher on the holiday in Wales. I met her at the funeral and she told me how much Lesley talked to her of home and wanting to get back to be with me.*]

Remember Lillian? [*At first it meant nothing, and then I remembered the day Lesley had had her waist-length hair cut, at the age of ten. Alan had teased her and said that he was going to call her 'George'. She had retorted if that was the case then she would call him 'Lillian'.*]

Alan and I returned home to the north not knowing what to think. Some of the things that Doris Stokes had said we found difficult to believe, but on the other hand there were details mentioned by 'Lesley' that even we had to dig deep into our memories to recall. I'm glad that I went. As a Christian I have always believed that Lesley is waiting in Heaven. The meeting with Doris Stokes confirmed my faith that my life sentence is worth seeing through as Lesley will be waiting for me.

A year or so later I attended a public session of Doris Stokes's in Sheffield. I went without giving Doris any indication that I would be there in the audience and sat near the back of the large hall. I was curious to see whether this woman really did make contact with those 'on the other side'. I wanted to put my private session with her in perpsective.

Half-way through her 'show' Doris suddenly stopped in a state of some perplexity. She turned to the audience and said, 'There's somebody who has been playing me up all night.' She looked up into the air and continued, 'Stop bothering me. Ann West isn't here today.'

I was astonished, to put it mildly. When I signalled that I was in fact in the hall Doris called me up on to the stage. We embraced and she gave me a large bunch of flowers – 'from Lesley'.

There have been voices of doubt raised in recent times about Doris Stokes's authenticity as a medium. I can only say that so far as I am concerned she was a most generous person and contact with her and Lesley gave me peace of mind in a way that no medication could ever have achieved. Her death from cancer in May 1987 meant the loss of a friend and a kind woman in a generally cold world.

Another death, but one which I have to admit caused me no grief, was that of Maureen Smith in 1980. She had been admitted to hospital with a brain tumour and was apparently beyond surgery. One evening we received an anonymous telephone call to tell us that the previous week Myra Hindley had visited her sister under escort from prison. She had arrived too late, for which news I'm afraid I was grateful. She who denied me the life of my daughter can expect no charity from me. Maureen Smith died alone at Crumpsall Hospital. The anonymous caller concluded by saying, 'If they let Myra go to the hospital they'll let her go to the funeral.'

I was furious. Why should a sadist who had tortured, killed and helped to bury innocent children in lost graves be shown compassion? Why should this beast who had posed for pictures on the graves of her victims and then picnicked on the very same spot be shown normal human decency? She was sub-human; to grant her such privileges was an affront to the memory of her victims. I determined that her attempt to attend the funeral at Moston crematorium should be unsuccessful. For the sake of Lesley's memory I would do what was necessary.

I arrived early with Wyn Pilkington and was followed shortly afterwards by John Kilbride's father. At least there were two parents who would show the authorities what they thought of such clemency for animals like Hindley. As soon as we arrived we knew that the anonymous tip-off had been correct. The area around the crematorium was swarming with police. Whom were all the motorcycle police and dog handlers and CID there to guard? The public had forgotten Maureen Smith. It was fifteen years since Brady and Hindley had been arrested.

A black limousine under police escort arrived first and a hard-faced woman who was obviously a wardress got out accompanied by a guard in plain clothes. I struggled to get closer as a second black limousine arrived. Police hands restrained me as I saw with horror a blonde-wigged woman start to get out. She was wearing a tailored suit and as I stared at her eyes I knew for sure . . . it was Myra Hindley. I screamed at her in rage as she stood staring at me with icy calm. There was not a flicker of emotion, just a cold, arrogant stare that chilled me to the very heart. It was the stare of a woman capable of destroying an innocent life by means of calculated physical and mental pain.

The police presence was too great. The party was safely inside the crematorium and the doors were closed and then locked. Trembling with rage, I released myself from the restraining hands of the police and wandered to the side of the building where some wreathes were being laid out for later inspection. I saw a wreath with a card saying 'To my beloved sister – from Myra'. I grabbed the wreath and shredded it into small pieces. If anyone had tried to interfere I think I would have killed him or her. Each shredded petal, each ripped leaf was for the screams and the pain and the agony Hindley and Brady had caused Lesley and John and Edward and all the others they had taken to cold, miserable graves on that terrible moor.

Eventually the service was over. The police presence increased around the door and the path to the waiting cars. I pressed forward, reaching into my handbag for the aerosol spray I had grabbed before leaving the house. It was a burn spray that a doctor had prescribed for me at some earlier date. I wanted to spray it into those cold eyes so that she could never again turn her contemptuous gaze upon the world. I wanted to blind the animal that had ruined so many lives. Suddenly I was grabbed and pinned against a wall by expert hands. I screamed to be set free. I demanded that I be let loose. I turned and stared at the scene unfolding by the limousines.

Poor old Patrick Kilbride was rushing towards the cars. Suddenly he was pinned to the ground by a plainclothes officer. A frail old man in his seventies was being floored by two younger men, with the odd punch and kick administered to keep him quiet. Once more the cold-eyed killer paused and gazed at the scene in disdain as she got back into one of the limousines. Myra had paid her last respects to her sister. Patrick Kilbride and I returned to our hopeless lives with a few more bruises but little satisfaction.

In 1987, as a result of reading about the luxurious conditions at maximum-security prisons, Alan and I went down to Cookham Wood prison in the south of England. This particular prison concerned us because it held Myra Hindley. I wanted her to know that whatever comfort she might be enjoying behind her fence there was somebody waiting for her.

Inevitably we ran into trouble as we approached. A photographer from a regional newspaper accompanied us to make a record of the conditions in which we suspected the prisoners lived. There was a wire fence, of course, but from what we could see the prison beyond the boundary looked more like a holiday camp. A prison officer came out and chased the photographer away (we were now on prison property). Alan and I stood our ground and refused to be so easily put off.

We walked along the walls of the prison, looking up at the windows, hoping that the evil bitch within could see me outside her lair. A uniformed official came out and explained that we would have to move off unless we wanted the police to be called. She spoke in a kind and polite manner and obviously knew who we were. I said that I wanted Myra Hindley to know that I was here, that I would always be waiting if she should ever get out, that I would always find her no matter where she was moved. The official patted me on the arm.

'She knows you're here, Mrs West. Don't worry, she knows you're here.'

I was satisfied. I had done my duty by Lesley. Later I wrote a letter to the Home Secretary giving him my opinions on maximum-security prisons. My own life sentence continues.

14

Before the disappearance of Lesley and the horrifying discoveries of ten months later I enjoyed good health. Although I developed pneumonia while pregnant with Brett in 1960 and discovered later that I had had a mild form of TB, I was not a person who visited the doctor very frequently. I was, I suppose, a tough northern lass. Looking back on that period I cannot believe I was so free of doctors, hospitals and constant medication. I have discovered over 25 years just how dangerous stress is to the human mind and body.

Perhaps if the tragedy of Lesley's murder had not taken place in the 1960s I would not have received the same medication and consequently would not be in the state in which I now find myself. That was the time when tranquillisers were viewed by doctors as the cure for all troubled minds. The dangers and long-term effects were discovered only later. The fact is that, although my current doctor is trying to reduce my intake of sedatives and sleeping tablets to manageable proportions, there has never been a day or a night in a quarter of a century when tablets have not been taken to make my waking hours tolerable and my nights a black pit of oblivion. I have lost the ability to control my own mind and body, my chemical dependence being almost total.

At first there was no doubt that sedatives were needed. A mother whose daughter has gone missing even for a short time will know what I mean. My daughter went missing for ten months. Her discovery and the details that then emerged made a continuation of drug treatment essential . . . or so the doctors thought. I certainly knew no better and was grateful, especially during the weeks when Brady and Hindley were on trial and the media was full of the horrors of their crimes. I attended court for a bare half-hour and my one statement was made through a solicitor. I think I had reached a point where my mind could no longer cope with the effort of confronting the truth. Nowadays there would be therapy, analysis, group encounter sessions. Then there was prescription after prescription, injection followed by tablets and yet more tablets. It was too easy, and there were too many. At first the doped-out sensation in which thought and memory faded was too attractive; the alternative of seeing Lesley's cruel, prolonged death constantly in my thoughts was too foul to bear. And then my body started to fight back. The effect of the tablets didn't last so long during the day; and at night sleep started to evade me despite the pills. I started to take more. A month's prescription would be finished in a fortnight and another prescription promptly issued. I chased pills with still more pills. I was becoming addicted at the NHS's expense.

Now the prescriptions are only issued a week at a time. This is not purely because of my abuse of medication but because of a very real fear on my doctor's part that it is dangerous for me to have too many pills in the house at the same time. In 1980 and 1982 I tried to take overdoses. It had all become too much. My body and mind had become so accustomed to the drugs that the horrors refused to leave me alone. The nightmares were with me continuously. Grotesque images from the mortuary and my imagination haunted me every hour. I had to escape from them. The sleep I sought was deep and permament.

Maybe now I am in greater control. Three 10-milligram tablets of Valium and two 100-milligram sleeping tablets per night are judged acceptable. When I was at my worst I barely functioned. Alan did his best to keep me going but I was spending most of the day in a walking trance. One of the consequences of this might well have been fatal. It was back in the 1970s and there was a bread shortage. Whatever the reason, it was particularly difficult in Manchester to get adequate supplies. We were then living in Chorlton and Alan had driven me to a bakery that we used. Having queued up and managed to get a couple of small loaves I was crossing the road when everything went black. The next thing I knew was four or five hours later when I found myself in hospital. Alan had to tell me what had happened.

Stepping out from behind a parked car to cross the road where Alan was waiting, I was hit by a car travelling at some speed. Apparently I went right up the bonnet and bounced off into the road. I was unconscious as I hit the tarmac. Alan had rushed across, got somebody to call for an ambulance, gathered up my purse and eventually travelled with me to the hospital. I'm told that my first reaction was to ask, 'Have you got the bread?' Maybe I was still in shock or perhaps the drugs had changed my sense of priorities. I demanded that Alan go immediately to the bakery to see where the bread was. When he asked the lady at the bakery if anyone had handed a couple of loaves in she declared that she had seen the whole incident, including a little old lady who picked the bread up from the road, put it in her basket and made a quick escape. Every cloud has a silver lining for someone, I suppose!

I suffered no long-term ill effects from being knocked down but the 'seventies saw another health problem arise which has lasted rather longer. For six months I had been consuming Rennies and other indigestion tablets at a prodigious rate. I thought it must be my cooking, yet the rest of the family seemed to be OK. Finally one day it became too much and I had to leave work at the Co-op Printers and return home, having rung the doctor. He came, examined me quickly and then instructed me to go straight to bed, to do no work and wait for the specialist that he would send round.

For some reason it came into my head that the stone slabs by the front door needed cleaning, especially if someone as grand as a specialist was coming. Instead of taking to my bed I grabbed a bucket and scrubbing brush and got down to some housework. About half an hour later a rather small man tapped me on the shoulder and said that he hoped I wasn't his patient. Within half an hour I was in Altrincham hospital where I was to remain for seven weeks. It transpired that my indigestion had been a heart attack! I was left with angina, which requires daily doses of nitro-glycerine tablets or a nitro spray. This was ten years after Lesley's disappearance.

Apart from developing asthma when bronchitis followed the heart operation, I remained in reasonable health for the next few years. I was still taking the tablets – there were quite a few of them now – and my struggle to keep Hindley behind bars gave me a will to live and a sense of purpose. As the 1980s progressed Alan tried his hardest to get me back into the mainstream of life. He was always thinking of ways to distract me from my morbid introspection, and there is no doubt that without him life would have been absolutely intolerable. The next stage in my body's revolt against the stress imposed upon it by fate and myself came in 1982. I can recall the time vividly as Alan and I were due to have a night out with my former husband Terry Downey and his wife.

We were going to see Russ Abbot performing at the Golden Garter nightclub in Wythenshawe and I must admit that I had been looking forward to being taken out of myself.

Just as we were ready to go I started to feel sick and developed stomach pains. Alan thought it might be nerves and suggested I have a drink, but I knew that a drink wouldn't help. I didn't want to spoil everybody else's evening, so I insisted that the rest of them go to the show. With some reluctance they finally left. The pains got no better, in fact they got considerably worse. I staggered up to bed with a hot-water bottle in the hope that they would go away. For a couple of hours they increased in intensity. I was sweating and in agony. Suddenly I heard Brett coming in and called out to him.

In a matter of minutes he had called for a doctor and before long an ambulance had arrived. I was being carried out to the ambulance when Alan arrived home. He followed the ambulance to the hospital and within half an hour I was undergoing emergency surgery. It turned out that I had cancer of the ovaries and was told later that if they hadn't operated I would have been dead within half an hour. I was about three weeks in Whythenshaw hospital and fortunately the cancer had not spread. I had been given yet another reprieve.

Only recently do doctors appear to have recognised the physical effects of mental stress. It seems quite clear in retrospect that my illnesses have been caused by the years of heartache, neurosis and horror. But it is not only the body that suffers. In 1982 I put myself into

Withington hospital's psychiatric unit in an attempt to wean myself off the sedatives and sleeping pills. The quality of my life had reached rock-bottom. I was going through the motions of living. I was merely existing. There was no pleasure or purpose in my life. Yet I wanted to return to the world.

A psychiatric unit is not the best place to go to feel uplifted. Surrounded by acloholics, schizophrenics and other nameless, terrible cases, I struggled to come to terms with my addiction. Instead of pills I was given exercises to perform which were designed to relax me physically. Instead of sleeping tablets I was given audio tapes of soothing music to help me drift off naturally. I'm ashamed to say that I spent more time having a quiet smoke with the ward sister in her office than doing my exercises or listening to my tapes. It was more depressing in the unit than at home. Having gone in voluntarily I discharged myself within a fortnight. At least the company at home was sane!

I tried to discipline myself with the pills. I struggled against the temptation to take them as a shield against my memories. But little by little I increased the dosage. I sought sleep constantly. Night was not enough. I wanted the pills to give me ease from the pain of memory in the daylight hours as well. Within two years I was worse than ever. Back I went to the psychiatric unit.

The treatment was the same. I got no better. I was put in front of a medical committee so that my needs and treatment could be discussed. After a long investigation I went back to the wards and discovered that my treatment was, if anything, harsher than before. Although I had my own room I was not allowed in it during the daytime in case I sought escape in sleep. I was forced to be in the day-room and in the constant, depressing company of patients in an even more distressing condition than I was. Not only was I haunted by the nightmares of my memory but my waking hours were spent in a mental hell as well. I discharged myself again. Maybe I had learned a lesson. I knew that if I kept on taking tablets at the rate I had been then I would probably end up in a place like Withington on an involuntary basis. I decided that I could never survive without sedatives and tranquillisers but that I would try to be disciplined in their use.

As the 25th anniversary of Lesley's departure from this world approaches fate has decided to tease me with yet another health problem. A chest x-ray at Withington hospital recently revealed 'an abnormality of the lung' and I was sent to a chest clinic in Manchester. On arrival there I was told by a doctor that Withington was 'passing the buck' and I would have to return there to have a diagnosis made. By now the uncertainty was beginning to make me panic. All I had been told was that there was an 'abnormality' – whatever that might mean. Back I went and eventually further tests revealed a dormant cancer on one lung. For some reason best known to medical science no operation can be performed until the cancer ceases to be dormant. In the meantime I struggle to give up smoking. There's no sense in giving fate all the trump cards.

Until I looked back objectively at all the illnesses over the years I had not realised quite how sick I have been. It is no wonder that Alan and the boys sometimes tease me with the name 'Bionic Woman'. It could all have been so different. We are not gifted with second sight, however. For all I know it might have been worse. Lesley and what happened to her has given me something to live for.

15

In the course of 25 years our experiences with the police and the press have revealed to Alan and me the best and worst of human behaviour. Some of the things that have been done and said to us over this period are almost unbelievable in what they reveal about the insensitivity of the human species. At other times we have sent up a silent prayer of thanks for the kindness and courtesy shown by those who went out of their way to try to ease our ever-present pain. They were all doing their jobs – both press and police . . . but there are many ways of doing a job, as we came to find out.

In the early days when it all began the press seemed to go berserk. Not a day went by from 27 December 1964, when Lesley went missing, to June 1965, when we were forced by press interference to move, without a knock on the door from someone wanting a story. The freelancers were the worst of all. At literally any time of day or night we could answer the door to discover standing there some hack journalist or freelance hopeful eager for an angle, a new twist, some tear-jerking item to satisfy 'the readers'.

For nearly six months Alan and I slept or dozed fitfully on the sofa and chairs in the sitting room. I cannot in all honesty say that we did this solely because of the constant attentions of the press. At first we were waiting for the sound of Lesley returning and we wanted to waste not a second in answering the door. We also waited desperately for any news from the police as to Lesley's whereabouts. But it was usually a reporter or, to be more accurate, a reporter accompanied by a photographer, who hammered on the door. For Alan it became a grim routine that had to be gone through time after time. I still find it hard to believe how unfeeling their behaviour was.

It was always the same: a knock on the door, which Alan would open, a flash from the photographer – 'Hello, it's Mr West, isn't it? I'd just like to talk to you about Lesley's disappearance. Can we come in?' At first we let them in, fondly believing that the publicity would somehow do Lesley some good. She had not been found and I firmly believed in my comfortable picture of some woman holding her prisoner. Perhaps our 'story' would be read by her and, conscience-stricken, she would release Lesley. In that first grim December and January there was a reporter of some sort on the doorstep virtually every five or ten minutes. I think we really believed at first that they were paying us such attention out of some genuine desire to help bring Lesley back.

The misquotes and sensationalism soon made us adjust our opinion. We came to feel we were being used. We came to feel dirty as the desire for titillating details overcame good taste. There was absolutely no news of Lesley, so 'human interest' had to fill the gap. The number of times reporters came close to being thrown off our balcony by Alan makes me tremble to recall. They could not have realised how near they were to featuring in their own stories! As I have said, the freelancers were the worst of all. They seemed to feel they had nothing to lose. Their irresponsibility was incredible. Two examples will serve to illustrate the point. They were by no means unique. I wish they were.

Three o'clock in the morning. I was dozing on the sofa. It was in the period when I still half-hoped to hear Lesley at the door. Sleep was fitful despite the fact that I was heavily sedated. Alan was sprawled in a chair trying to switch his mind off and get some rest. I heard loud banging at the front door. As I struggled to get my senses together I heard Alan unlocking the door. I heard a drunken voice loudly demanding that Alan should let him in as he wanted to speak to Mrs Downey. By the time I had staggered into the hall Alan was letting this Fleet Street reject know precisely where he could put his notebook and what would be done to him if he ever pulled such a stunt again. Much the worse for drink, the reporter persisted. That was one who got very close to taking the short way down from our first-floor flat to the ground.

A particularly hideous example of a sick mind at work presented itself to us at roughly the same period. It was daytime, I think. I was in such sedated state that days, nights, weeks and months merged in harrowing confusion. Alan answered the door as usual and returned with a puzzled expression on his face. I tried to focus on the stranger who accompanied him into the room. I knew the face. I had seen this slim, elegant man somewhere before. Suddenly the face and a name out of my drug-blurred mind made a match. I had seen his films on television . . . Emlyn Williams. What was *he* doing here! He left us in no doubt.

'I'm doing some research on Lesley's background. It's a writing project I'm on. She had to sleep with her brothers, didn't she? Not much room in these council flats, is there?'

Alan's face went ominously white. He dragged Williams's coat by the sleeve and dragged him upstairs to show him her empty room and then as quickly dragged him downstairs again. With an angry glint in his eye the fading 'star' informed us that if we wouldn't give him a story he'd make up his own.

I left Lesley's light burning for six months, but it seemed to attract some very strange creatures indeed. It also attracted a few genuine journalists, men who still respected their craft and those who gave them their stories. One name stands out from the few who earned our respect – Trevor Reynolds. Although only young, probably little more than twenty, he was a real gentleman. He was already working for the *Daily Herald* and never treated us with anything but courtesy and respect. The articles he turned in were incisive, well written and courageous. If only there could have been more like him.

As for the rest, Alan and I felt some of them must have crawled out from under some very slimy stone. Yet the worst of the breed certainly left no stone unturned in pursuit of a new slant on our misery. Even Terry, who had returned to Holland Street School in January, was not immune from their attentions. A reporter actually turned up at the school asking for Terry to try to get a story out of him. Fortunately the headmaster was shrewd enough to put a stop to that, but it was not the only time that the children were sought out to be pressed for inside information. It all seems such a waste of time and energy. What could they have said? – 'We are miserable. We are lost without Lesley. We want our Lesley back.' All that would have been true but insufficiently sensational.

They came from all over. The period between the finding of Lesley's body on Saddleworth Moor and her burial brought them crawling out of the woodwork. Even though we had moved to the new overspill housing estate at Hattersley they still tracked us down.

One afternoon in that terrible period between Lesley's body being found on the moors and her funeral there was another knock on the door. There they stood, the inevitable reporter and photographer, but this time the accent was German. I stood in the hallway as Alan explained that we did not wish to see anybody at this time. Still they persisted.

'But we have come specially from Germany.'

'I can't help that.'

'We are from *Bild* magazine. We can pay.'

'I'm sorry. We are not interested.'

'Perhaps you would be prepared to come to the moor with us. We would like to take some photos of Mrs Downey at the place where Lesley was buried.'

I could sense Alan's hackles rising. He was struggling to keep cool.

'Ah, is that Mrs Downey behind you?'

I retreated further down the hall. I saw the German journalist's partner raise his camera and aim it at me from the doorstep where Alan was keeping them at bay. He had made a grave mistake. With a snarl Alan knocked his expensive camera to the ground and told the pair of them what he thought of journalists, Germans and photographers in very clear terms. They scuttled away with their tails between their legs.

The love-hate relationship we had with such types is illustrated by the strange fact that later that day the same pair returned and apologised for their insensitive behaviour. They even insisted on taking us out for a drink and a meal. I still cannot believe it, but we ended up giving them a bed for the night before they returned to Germany the next day. Grief brings one strange friends. It came into my mind later that perhaps they *did* get their story, but at least we had made our point.

Considering how expensive the ruined camera had appeared to be, it would have been a costly little story if it was ever written.

On another occasion in that terrible week another pair turned up on the doorstep, this time from America. They had been sent from *Time* magazine to cover the story. They too wanted me to go up on to the moors to have photographs taken at the site of Lesley's lonely grave. Again they were soon relieved of their illusions that such a story, and certainly such photographs, would be possible. Now, almost 25 years later, I detest even a distant glimpse of the moors. I would never have posed at that horrifying place. The front-door argument took less than five minutes to conclude. Yet there was a strange ending to the incident years later.

Our eldest son, Terry, had joined the Merchant Navy and was on a boat headed for Montreal. One evening he idly picked up an old magazine to flick through during an off-duty spell. Suddenly he paused. Turning the pages, he came across a feature on the Moors Murders and found Lesley's face staring at him. Hundreds of miles from home in the middle of the North Atlantic he turned to the cover. It was *Time* magazine. Perhaps they had written their exclusive story after all . . . but it was not with our help. A funny breed, journalists.

Television has always treated us more fairly and with greater responsibility. Brian Trueman and Eric Robson, the co-presenters of *Brass Tacks* on BBC2, were the essence of courtesy and fair-mindedness. The experience of appearing live on that show has been described in a previous chapter, but I came away from the studios with a strong belief in the impartiality and sensitivity of this branch of the media. Perhaps it has something to do with there being less pressure on them to be sensational and to get sales, or viewers, at all costs.

The police, too, have generally been good to us. Even those who in the first few days gave us such a hard time were only doing their job. Their methods can be forgiven given that their one concern was for Lesley. That we had in common. No amount of training can prepare a policeman for dealing with people like ourselves, driven mad by sorrow. No case can have been like ours – so harrowing in its detail and macabre in its execution. On the whole they tried their best to avoid stepping too clumsily on our distracted feelings. They did not always succeed, but at least they tried.

The senior officers with whom we have come into contact over the years have been marvellous. Since at one point the police of five different areas were searching for Lesley and the beasts that had taken her we had contact with a good few CID and uniformed officers. My first meeting with Bob Talbot was in unfortunate circumstances, to put it mildly. It was his task to play me the extract from that awful tape in order to identify Lesley's voice. It was his responsibility to introduce me via that hideous recording to the depths of human depravity as practised by the bitch Hindley. He had a child of his own, a daughter little older than Lesley was, and I now realise what he had gone through listening to the whole of those seventeen minutes of Hell over and over again. I don't think we ever met without his apologising to me for putting me through that.

He was a tall, plain-spoken, serious man. His blue eyes were always calm but penetrating. I learned later that he had only recently been promoted from a post with the CID to the rank of Superintendent of the Stalybridge division. It was he who had actually gone into that sordid house in Hattersley and found Brady, Hindley and the hacked corpse of Edward Evans. It was he who had found the ticket to the left-luggage office at Central Station and drew back the curtain on the monsters' reign of terror. He always spoke calmly and with great care. His accent was of the North and he never failed to impress both Alan and me with his quiet dignity.

Arthur Benfield was a contrast to Bob Talbot. A middle-aged bachelor, rosy-faced and starting to lose his hair, he seemed to me to have a sense of humour. He was a dependable, no-nonsense type. Only a week before Brady and Hindley were arrested he had been made Detective Chief Superintendent for Cheshire. He certainly was pitched in at the deep end. When he retired a few years ago the force lost a great policeman. He was always completely open with us. He must have understood our need for facts in a case that held so many terrible mysteries. He came round to the house at Bowden Close a number of times to see how we were coping. 'If you want to know anything . . . if you want to talk . . .' There was no secrecy or reserve with Arthur Benfield; you always knew where you were with him.

John Stalker was a quietly spoken, young detective sergeant when he first became involved with our case. Together with other detectives, he worked hour after hour and day after day enquiring from door to door about possible sightings of Lesley in the district. We never found him anything but patient, understanding and supportive as the days became weeks and, ultimately, months. Closely involved in the search for Lesley, he remained a visitor to the house and continued investigations long after the other policemen had been assigned to other duties.

It was to be many years before our paths crossed again. We met quite recently at a book signing in Manchester following the publication of his autobiography. I held out his book for him to sign and he looked up. There was instant recognition in his eyes and a sad smile. We hugged each other silently in the middle of the crowded bookshop, oblivious of others around. So much had happened over the intervening years. I remember him saying that I should write *my* story next and I laughed. But he had sown a seed in my mind . . .

Although I also had dealings with Peter Topping it was in different circumstances. He was a difficult man to get close to. I got the impression that he wouldn't let his left hand know what his right was doing. He was clearly a clever man and involved in a desperate and devious bid to get Brady to reveal the sites of other graves on the moors. Perhaps it was the fact that we were both trying to do the same thing in different ways that prevented us from becoming friends, or even particularly close.

It was Geoff Rimmer who will perhaps remain in my heart and memory the longest. A charming man, polite and sensitive, he never came to the house without explaining how the case was going or asking how we were getting on. Over the years we have stayed in contact and he has been generous and free with his advice. Whenever we have had trouble with the press over misquotes or biased features it has been Geoff Rimmer who has tried to help or put us on the right track He has always told us that the press are too strong to fight but always adds with a twinkle in his eye that it's still worth trying. I guess we feel close to Geoff Rimmer because he shares our determination that for monsters like Brady and Hindley imprisonment must be for life.

The press and the police . . . for 25 years Alan and I have been involved with them in one way or another. We have had time to come to terms with the way our lives have been affected in so many ways by our long-term relationship. We have never ceased to wish, despite having met some good men, that our lives had been too quiet and uneventful to have brought either group of people into them.

16

It took months of soul-searching and heartache. Night after night, I tossed and turned in my bed as the voice pounded in my tormented mind. 'You have to do it. You owe it to Lesley.'

Alan was all for it. But he deliberately took a step back. He explained the decision had to be mine and mine alone. He wasn't opting out, simply making sure I was satisfied, in my own mind, that, having made the decision to start a correspondence with Brady, I could carry it on to the bitter end. Even the thought of writing to the man who butchered my lovely Lesley made my stomach churn. But the voice convinced me – it had to be done. I had to face the biggest challenge of my tormented life.

It took every ounce of courage and determination in

my fragile body to pick up the pen. I looked at the blank piece of paper and saw Brady's evil eyes staring back at me. Suddenly, it was all too much. I threw the pen contemptuously across the room. Alan, patient as always, walked across, picked it up and put it down in front of me. Twice more I tried. And twice the pen was hurled away in sheer disgust.

Alan slipped his arms around my shoulders, calmed me down again, and whispered soothingly: 'If it is going to upset you so much, forget it. He's not worth it.'

But the voice came back, insistent, demanding, irresistible.

'You owe it to Lesley.'

Slowly, deliberately, I wrote my first words to Brady: 'Dear Mr Brady, I am the mother of the little girl you murdered.'

It is still difficult to describe exactly why I wrote those words. At first, I suppose it was a desperate desire to know – to be reassured in some way that Lesley had not suffered unduly. But that can't be it. I knew how she had suffered. I had heard that sickening tape recording, seen the evidence with my own eyes. I suppose I hoped that something, somehow, would emerge to console me – to give me hope that it had not been quite so bad as my imagination feared it must have been. It was to prove, inevitably, I realise now, a forlorn hope.

I only realised, as I began to write, that, incredible as it may seem, Brady might still be able to help me. It was his confession to the murder of two other youngsters, Pauline Reade and Keith Bennett, which triggered the idea. In a way, I considered myself lucky. At least Lesley's body had been found. She'd had a decent, Christian burial and I had a comforting place I could go to each day to tend, lovingly, with plants and flowers – and remember. The families of Pauline and Keith had no such place.

I wanted those kiddies found. Their grieving families deserved that. Brady could tell me where they were. So I deliberately set out to gain his confidence – no matter what the cost, and persuade him to reveal where they were buried.

I wrote: 'Seeing as you never want parole and want to die in prison, please tell me where Pauline and Keith are so we can give them a proper burial.'

And I added: 'You destroyed my life when you killed Lesley, so at least bring a little happiness back for me and help find the other children.'

And I asked: 'Can we meet and talk?'

As I sealed the envelope, I turned to Alan and said: 'I don't expect he will reply.'

The days passed into weeks without response and I became more and more convinced I would hear nothing.

It was nearly six weeks later that we heard the post drop through the front door and Alan went to collect it. He came into the lounge with a bundle of letters in his hand. There were five in all. Two were junk mail, two bills. The fifth was a small, cheap, white envelope with a Liverpool post mark. Alan's swarthy face turned pale and he couldn't stop his hand from shaking as he said: 'This is it. The bastard has replied'.

I shivered from head to toe. This was what I had been waiting and hoping for. But now it had finally appeared, nothing in the world could persuade me to open that letter. I just could not bring myself to touch anything which had been written by the hand which killed my little girl.

Slowly, Alan tore open the envelope, unfolded the letter inside and began to read, his voice shaky, faltering, drying up with emotion. It was dated April 14, 1986, and it began: 'Dear Mrs West . . .'

Brady wrote: 'You had no need to assure me you meant no harm in wanting to visit. It pained me that you felt the need for such an assurance, as you have every right to wish me harm.'

He said the prison authorities would not allow me to visit him because the 'gutter press' would exploit, distort and invent sensational stories.

He also wrote: 'You know beyond doubt that I have stated I have never applied for parole and never shall. I can assure you personally of the remorse I feel, but I prefer action to words.

'I've spent the last 18 years doing braille work, transcribing books into braille for schools. I know I can't balance the past, of course, but at least I can do something positive and useful. The satisfaction I get from doing this is beyond measure.'

And he revealed: 'I kept your letter on top of my table as a constant reminder. It has taken me weeks to reply because I couldn't find the words that cover pain and further distress. I only knew I had to answer.'

It was the start of an amazing correspondence which was to last over five years, in which we chatted about the weather, family problems and illnesses and the real, underlying reason for it all – the hidden bodies on the moors.

Between May and August of 1986 Brady wrote to me three times. In each letter he complained bitterly about the way Dave Smith has been treated with such leniency by the police. His insistence that there is a cover-up to repay Smith for having turned Queen's Evidence is obsessive. In this case it is an obsession that I can share. I am convinced that the terrible events of that Boxing Day took place with the help of others.

At this period Smith was writing to Brady repeatedly at the Park Lane Hospital in Liverpool. Smith was writing but Brady was not reading – or so he told me. I would be intrigued to know what Brady's former partner-in-crime had to say to him. The Smith letters were apparently returned unopened and unread. In Brady's third letter he claims, rather ironically in my opinion, that he almost vomited when he recalled extracts from Smith's diaries that were read out in court during the trial. He quotes phrases such as 'Murder is a hobby', 'Religion is a cancer' and 'Rape is a state of mind'. The irony of Brady's alleged reaction lies in the thought that Smith had almost certainly learned this sick philosophy from Brady himself.

In some letters Brady strikes a lighter note. He writes to me for example of a visit made to the wards by Jimmy Saville. For me it is painful to visualise that larger-than-life media personality laughing and shaking hands with my child's murderer. It made me angry that someone so much associated in the public mind with good works, and helping children in particular, should have been brightening Brady's existence.

A curious episode occurred between these last three letters and the next, when Alan and I paid a visit to Brady's mother. As usual the press was involved. I read one Sunday morning an article in a national newspaper that referred to Ian Brady's mother as 'a frail, half-blind old lady'. Coincidentally, Maggie Enfield of the *Daily Mail* rang a day or so later to ask if I would like to see Brady's mother. Since I knew that she had not brought up her son, having had to have him fostered at an early age, I decided that I would like to meet her. In a strange sort of way we were both long-term victims of her son's actions.

Alan and I went to Mrs Brady's house in Chorlton-on-Medlock with Maggie Enfield. When the door was opened to us we were astonished. We had expected the 'frail, half-blind old lady' of the newspaper report. Instead we were greeted by a very strong-looking woman of above-average height who seemed in good health and was far from being half-blind. We should not have been surprised after all the years of reading rubbish about ourselves in newspapers.

We talked together and Mrs Brady gave us tea. After a while Maggie Enfield left us to file her story. Once we were alone with Brady's mother we got on quite well and she opened her heart to us. She was genuinely ill-informed about most of the details of her son's case and his relationship with Myra Hindley. She hadn't read many of the papers and said later that she had learned more from Alan and me that day than she had in the previous twenty years. She occasionally received letters from her son and showed us a tray on the wall that had been sent to her by Ian as a gift from prison. It hadn't actually been made by him: he had got another prisoner to make it for her. The gesture seemed somehow typical of Brady and summed up in many ways the gulf that lies between mother and abandoned son.

She invited us to visit her again and said that she would mention to Ian that we had been to see her the next time she wrote to him. We were about to leave when Alan noticed that there was a photographer lurking by the front door. Somehow the news of our visit had got out and the inevitable freelance 'chancer' was waiting opportunistically for his lucrative shot. Alan suggested to Mrs Brady that she should go back in. There was no reason why this woman who had had the misfortune of giving birth to Ian Brady should have her life made more miserable by such publicity. The photographer was annoyed but asked Alan and me to pose in the doorway. Alan pushed him away and fortunately for the photographer he did not pursue the matter.

Amazingly, perhaps, we had felt no resentment towards Brady's mother. She had not brought him up. She had not contributed to the evil in his nature. She was a victim of circumstance and had clearly suffered in some ways for what for what her son had done. It cannot be pleasant going through life bearing a name that is notorious and will always be associated with the ultimate in sadism.

In June 1987 Brady responded to my letter in which, amongst other things, I said that I had visited his mother. He was clearly distracted by events concerning the renewed search for the missing bodies on the moors as his mother was only mentioned in a brief postscript. Brady seems to have been in an excited mood and the prospect of the case being re-opened distracted him, for one reason or another, from day-to-day concerns: 'I suppose you've seen or heard,' he wrote, 'that the Home Office, on the strength of my information, are re-opening the case. I can't tell you anything else. You'll see or read about it soon.'

I took this at first to mean that Brady was simply looking forward to helping the police with the search for grave sites on Saddleworth Moor. It was not so simple as that.

In November of 1987 I received a letter from Brady in which he described a futile visit to the moors arranged for him by the police and in which he also referred self-pityingly to the exhaustion the all-day search caused him.

> Before I'd received your letter, I had already seen Mr Topping twice in the past two weeks, studying a video and the RAF photos taken from 10,000 feet. But they were of little help and no substitute for being on the moor itself and I told Mr Topping so.

The police got me on to the moor at four in the morning to avoid the crowd of reporters who were sleeping in their cars up there. We spent the next 12 hours searching the rough country. At 4.30 p.m. in the afternoon we stopped to eat. I pointed out to Mr Topping that we had at least another 4 hours of daylight left, but he said that security arrangements had already been made to get me back to the hospital. I later discovered that the medical team escorting me had told Mr Topping that I was mentally and physically exhausted.

What the letter also contains are a number of remarks and accusations regarding Smith which – to put it mildly – do nothing to allay our concern.

It is possible that Brady's anger and accusations are caused by his frustration at not being able to identify the grave site, and by his losing out in the 'race' with Hindley to achieve more publicity. It is equally possible that Brady is becoming increasingly bitter, as the years pass, about Smith's continued freedom if he feels him to be guilty.

In conclusion Brady turns to the subject of four further murders about which he has informed Peter Topping – a man and a woman in Manchester and two other individuals in Scotland. Whether or not this insistence on setting the record straight is an attempt on Brady's part to salve what might pass as his conscience, the police seem to have taken alarmingly little notice of his admissions.

Brady's letter of December 1987, to Alan, is fairly

9th/12/87   490, I. Brady,
            Park Lane Hospital,
            Liverpool.

Dear Mr West,
                    I've just come
back from the moors and I
wish to get developments down
while still fresh in my mind. But
first I'll deal with a point in
your letter, and in your wife's.
I showed Mr Topping the letter of
your wife's stating that Mr Topping
had said to her to be careful
not to be conned by information.
Mr Topping denies having said
that to you or Mrs West.
    I got no warning when my
door was opened at five o'clock
this morning and I was told that
the police were coming to collect

                        P.T.O.

164

2

me. I had been trying non-stop from July to get back to the moor, yet the Home Office dragged its feet till December and the shortest day of the year. When we got to the moor everything was covered by frost and frozen water. But it was all worth it because within an hour I rectified the big mistake that had been made. And when I saw it I felt a great surge of relief and satisfaction. It greatly reduced the search area to a spot where a sheep pen is and a junction of two streams. I know without any doubt

3

that the gully and the area I
was searching is there. When
spent the rest of the day trying
to locate the precise spot but I
~~was~~ zigzagging up and down
logically in order to make sure I
didn't miss anything. Mr Topping
gave me plenty of support and
allowed me to go wherever I
spotted something, or possibilities. But
I was racing against time and had to
keep hurrying before the early
darkness fell.
On the return journey in the van I
asked Mr Topping what he intended to
do next. He said the weather was
too "inclement" at the moment and

that _no search would_ be organised. I
was deflated by this — if it was good
enough to take one there it should
be good enough for a search. I'd
like to see forty or fifty policemen
on that slope ~~digging~~ tackling _every_
gully.
    I'm grateful for all the help you
gave me to get back there. And it
wasn't wasted — _I know_ it's there.
And I've no intention _of_ letting go
of the matter until I find, or the
police find, that gully. And I'll
continue to need any help from you.
        Sincerely,
                    Ian Brady

self-explanatory but certainly highlights the 'difficulties' that had arisen in the relationship between himself, Peter Topping and ourselves (*see* pp. 164–7).

Brady refers to a visit that Alan and I had had from Peter Topping, about which I had told him in a letter. Topping and his hatchet-faced assistant Frank Provost had called to try to insist that they be allowed to vet any letters passing between me and Brady. I had told Topping that Brady had sent me a letter in which he indicated that he knew where Keith Bennett's body was. At this point Topping had sneered and told me Brady was conning me. Topping's denial, mentioned by Brady in his second paragraph, of what he had said to us about who was conning whom, confirms the feeling Alan and I share that sometimes the police were so intent on not letting the right hand know what the left was doing that they wasted precious opportunities. During that particular visit Topping had accused us of spoiling the special relationship he had been developing with Brady. But I remain convinced that the relationship I might have developed with my child's killer was more likely to prove productive than any that a policeman might have established.

The final paragraph of the above letter, expressing Brady's thanks for help in getting back on the moor, is perhaps the best justification I can give for the strange correspondence between myself and my child's killer. On that occasion the search was fruitless but the focus of the search for Keith Bennett's grave is narrowing.

Perhaps one of the strangest letters I have received

from Brady arrived in early January 1988. The bulk of the contents was familiar enough – the usual denials that he was blocking my attempts to talk to him in hospital, the complaints about Peter Topping's handling of the search on the moors.

What suddenly struck deep into my heart was the final paragraph in which he hoped I would not be offended if he wished me a happy and peaceful New Year. I stared at this in disbelief, rage and nausea gripping me deep in my guts. Why was this pleasantry so sickening? Why were my hands shaking as they held the note?

This creature who had taken my daughter away from me so many years ago had had the effrontery to wish me a happy and peaceful New Year from his prison hospital at the turning of another year.

I sobbed quietly in self-pity, contemplating yet another long year in this lonely world totally devoid of peace and happiness.

In February 1988 Brady returned again to the matter of his failure to find the lost graves on the moor. His ego is in evidence once again as he seems to take pleasure in setting John Stalker against Peter Topping over the question of a winter search of Saddleworth.

> You'll recall I criticised Mr Topping for taking me to the moor in December, which has the shortest days of the year, was the worst for me psychologically and had the most uncertain weather (5 degrees below zero in my particular case). Well, now Stalker, in his book [Stalker, *published in February 1988*], also criticised Mr Topping for his choice of December. So

> it wasn't just me. The situation re police cover-ups in the other killings I mentioned (two in Manchester, one in Glasgow, one at Loch Long) still remains the same.

His final remark about the alleged 'cover-up' by the police of the other killings for which he claimed responsibility chilled me. Unless the police have definite evidence to the contrary surely they should follow up Brady's claims?

The eventual discovery of Pauline Reade's body in its shallow grave on Saddleworth Moor in early 1988 was to elicit a particularly lengthy letter from Brady. The fact that it was with Myra Hindley's help – not his – that Pauline's body was found seems to have prompted his protracted response. Once again Brady reveals his egotistical desire to be always in the right, at the expense of others. Both his ex-partner in murder *and* Peter Topping come in for detailed criticism in this letter of April 1988.

His mind, jealous of Hindley's 'publicity' in leading the police to Pauline's grave, seems to be focusing determinedly on the issue of the other four murders to which he has made so many previous references. I now begin to wonder if it is the pricking of a conscience or a desire to rival Hindley in gaining publicity for himself that triggers his repeated references to the murders in Manchester and Scotland. Whatever his motive Brady's claims surely deserve investigation. If Brady is telling me the truth an innocent man may be still in prison.

I know precisely what I'm looking for and so does Hindley. But she simply took the police to the general area re Pauline Reade when in fact she could've taken them to the *precise* spot. And she didn't bother to tell the police that clumps of grass had been torn up and transplanted on the site to hide it, so the police took weeks to find it, and even then I think it was pure luck – either that or Hindley became impatient with the police bungling around and told them of the transplanted grass.

Re the other murders – the following *facts* are a description of the *real* situation. *After* I was arrested in 1965 the police, the chiefs of five different forces, interrogated me about the man killed on the wasteground near Piccadilly and Ardwick Green, months *before* my arrest and *after* his death. M and I refused to answer any questions.

He then goes on to elaborate upon what he believes to be a systematic police cover-up in order to 'clear the books' and the 'fitting-up' of someone else with false evidence. He subsequently continues to accuse the police of bungling the three other murder cases: the woman dumped in the canal in Manchester and passed off as a suicide, and the two victims in Scotland, one shot, one stabbed.

Brady's mood in this letter is even more vindictive than normal and Peter Topping comes in for considerable criticism. Brady claims that there will be no further searches on the moors for the body of Keith Bennett, for reasons of 'economics' and 'politics', and that although he – Brady – has offered full co-operation

25/7/88

Dear Mrs Downey,

Thank you for your last letter.
I had already seen the cutting you sent. You
will notice that the report mentions no names, ie,
"a police spokesman said."
I've written to the Chief Constable, Anderton.
The reply I got is very carefully phrased
and gives away nothing. He is sitting on
the fence :-
"... a report was submitted to the Director
of Public Prosecutions concerning a number
of matters you claimed responsibility for
both in the Greater Mcr area and
Scotland. Having considered the file
the D.P.P. reached a decision based on the
evidence available and the attendant
circumstances and Mr Topping has told
me that he acquainted you with the outcome

of those considerations."

Mr Topping acquainted me of nothing.
And Anderton's letter carefully neglects
to put in writing anything about a
decision. It tells nothing at all.
You must understand my position. I am
in captivity until I die, so why should
I bother fighting a police cover-up
of charging the wrong man; calling
the canal case suicide; saying ~~then~~ that the
Glasgow records don't go back to the
1960s; and the Scottish police
searching (1965/66) along Loch
Lomond instead of Loch Long?
The list of police blunders is so
farcical that I don't blame them ~~for~~ for
wanting to leave things as they are.
As for my two visits to the moors.
The first took me completely by

3

surprise. I did not ask to go, not was I given any warning. I said that I would only take half an hour and that I had no wish to wait around. But, after 23 years inside, the moor looked all different to me and destroyed my concentration. The second visit again took place without any warning, six months later and when the police knew in advance that I did not wish to go back up there in December as those are the shortest daylight hours of the year, and the moor was under ice at 5 degrees below zero. I argued with the police two hours, but I was told that, if I didn't go there, I wouldn't get another chance. So, I had no choice but to go up. I know I can pinpoint K.B. to a distance of twenty paces. The police have bungle

4 ..

it twice. Again, ~~why~~ *why* should I fight the
police or ~~Home~~ Office reluctance to
give me the opportunity to close the case?
I want it closed, that's why! ~~&~~ fight.
The whole situation is a farce, what
with this red-herring about Hindley
and hypnosis, etc. It's all just ~~over~~ an
excuse, a diversion — a cheap P.R.
gimmick to avoid doing the obvious.

I'm not getting sufficient medication
at present and my concentration is
sporadic. Again, I can't understand
why they don't want me to think
clearly — which I do if I'm ~~given~~ *given*
enough medication to enable me
to relax and concentrate. I think
it is the Home Office which wishes me
destroyed mentally, especially my memory.

Sincerely, I.S. Brady

175

Peter Topping has turned him down. I can understand that mounting a security operation to allow Brady on to the moors again would be costly, but what 'politics' has to do with it is beyond me.

Brady's next letter revealed that his excitement was caused by what he believed would be a chance either to unburden himself of the guilt of further murders or to embarrass the police. I suspect it was both. Brady was still trying to get the police to accept that he had committed two hitherto unpublicised murders in Scotland and two more in Manchester. In the Manchester cases a woman's body found in the canal had been judged a suicide, while a mental defective had been found guilty of the murder of a second individual whose body was found on waste ground near Piccadilly. Brady seemed to relish the prospect of further headlines connecting him with these incidents.

In July 1988 I received a further letter from Brady (*see* pp 172–5). I had sent him a newspaper cutting which reported the police's decision not to pursue any further investigations into the other cases for which Brady claimed responsibility. The shaky handwriting of the original and the writer's paranoid protests about receiving insufficient medication tell their own story. Obsession with these other murders had gripped him for a whole year.

Readers will appreciate what my feelings must have been when I read Brady's assurance that he accepts a life sentence is for life. I was, however, thoroughly alarmed at Brady's reference again to a police cover-up and the charging of the wrong man for a murder in Manchester. Since Brady gains no advantage from claiming responsibility for this and other murders I shudder at the thought of another person serving time for an act of savagery of which he may well be innocent. Brady's arrogance is often in evidence in our correspondence. He is frequently scornful of the police, accusing them of 'incompetence', while boasting of his own superiority. Media stories that Hindley was having hypnosis in prison to help her recall the grave site of Keith Bennett had aroused Brady's contempt; his scathing remarks about his ex-partner in crime clearly reveal the bitter rivalry that has developed between them. My correspondence, together with the newspaper cuttings I sent Brady, helped to stimulate their desire to beat each other to identifying the lost graves.

Although he is probably too sick to be aware of the cruel irony of his final paranoid remark (about the Home Office's alleged desire to 'destroy his memory'), the phrase struck me a heart-rending blow. While he complains about what he believes are attempts to wipe away his memory, the mothers and fathers of the children he and his partner destroyed are haunted daily by memories of the offspring they will never see again. Brady's letters stir reactions he could never comprehend.

By August 1988 the target of Brady's fury seems to have shifted to Chief Constable Anderton. Since Anderton's views on society's delinquents and villains are well known, perhaps Brady decided to 'take on' this epitome of respectability with accusations that put the police in general and Anderton in particular in a very poor light.

> I received a visit without warning from Det. Chief Inspector Knuffer [*Topping's assistant*] today. It is now clear that it was *Chief Constable Anderton* who stopped the search for Keith Bennett and halted the investigation of the other two cases in the Manchester area.
>
> He *personally* has also refused a request made by both myself and my solicitor for a copy of the so-called 'tartan album', a copy of which Anderton has.
>
> In short, Anderton is the one *personally blocking* all investigations and hindering both myself and Mrs Bennett by *withholding co-operation and evidence*.
>
> Why has no one informed Stalker that I'll speak to him?
>
> Would you please enlist the help of MP's re all the above matters? I am doing so also.

The question of the notorious 'tartan album' comes up again in later correspondence. Brady believes that this album, containing photographs and other material, will settle the question of the other murders once and for all. It may be that he is bluffing and just searching for material to make the police look fools or villains. It may be that the album does contain evidence which would allow justice finally to be done. The question of the 'tartan album' should, in the interests of justice, be resolved as soon as possible.

The reference to John Stalker is an indication of

Brady's willingness to help in the search for Keith Bennett, despite Anderton and Topping's apparent lack of interest.

As December 1988 approached I received a particularly disturbed letter from Brady. Perhaps this was because he tends to be in a particularly 'poor' psychological state at the close of the year, or maybe circumstances were building up to frustrate him. He is clearly still brooding over the 'advantage' he feels Hindley has gained in the earlier location of Pauline Reade.

> When I discovered that M. H. had been deliberately misleading the police by 'distancing' herself from the sites by not giving the *precise* locations which she knows and knew, I felt deep anger, in view of the efforts I had made in the worst conditions.
>
> She, as I predicted to the police, still wishes to impress the Parole Board by appearing to help the police while at the same time suggesting her innocence by pretending not to know the precise locations.

His reference to Myra Hindley and the Parole Board yet again makes my flesh creep.

The campaign against Chief Constable Anderton continues unabated further on in the letter. It is almost as if all Brady's hatred and anger has become focused on this 'pillar of the establishment'. He certainly wants some questions answering.

There is a certain matter which you may be able to bring pressure on. I wrote a recorded-delivery letter to Chief Constable James Anderton *three months* ago asking him:

(A) Please confirm in *writing* that you *personally* halted the search for Keith Bennett.

(B) Please confirm in *writing* that you *personally* halted further investigations into the deaths of Veronica Bondi (Moss Side 1963), Ben Marsden (1959) and Wm Cullen (1964).

(C) Please confirm in *writing* that you *personally* refused to take action against a bogus 'Dr' Keaton who wrote to me about hypnosis, sold the letter to a popular daily paper and then conspired with that paper in the false claim that I wrote the letter to them.

(D) Please confirm in *writing* that you *personally* refused to let me have a photocopy of the 'tartan album' which is my property for reference purposes.

The tartan album has clearly become an obsession with Brady. In March 1989 Brady comments in a letter to me that he believes the police are now trying to cover up the embarrassing fact that they have either lost the notorious album or permitted it to be stolen by a member of the force who has sold it to a well-known and usually respectable Sunday newspaper.

My bizarre correspondence with Brady and Hindley has always been carried out with a purpose in mind. The police have interfered in the process but I am convinced, as are some journalists, that it was Brady's communication with me that caused Hindley to unlock yet another gruesome secret from her past. So some good has come of it all. Pauline Reade now rests in a decent grave. Maybe Keith Bennett will be rescued from the moor before too long. Maybe the letters still contain undiscovered clues.

Yet I feel a cold shiver at what is conspicuously absent from *all* Brady's correspondence – the slightest sign of remorse for the dead children whose graves he has sought.

But the correspondence continues. Who knows why? Who can say why my daughter's killer feels the need to write to the mother whose life he destroyed as surely as he destroyed her child's? Who can say why *I* need to continue this traumatic communication with the last person to see Lesley alive? I suspect that we will go on with our letters till one or other of us dies. How strange and how pathetic – two people with so little, yet so much, in common, forever linked by this succession of letters.

Postscript

Around the middle of 1989, there was press speculation that Brady was to apply for parole. In view of his previous comments to me, I wrote asking him about this.

His letter back, in August, stated categorically: 'I have never sought freedom, nor do I wish it . . . I shall die in captivity by my own choice.' And he added: 'In fact, I have only contempt for the outside world and it holds as much interest for me as a putrid apple. I would not even accept it as a gift.'

Shortly after, I received a letter from a Liverpool press agency, who were acting for Brady, asking if I had any objection to him writing a book on the murders. Alan and I talked it over at length and decided we would agree on two conditions. One was that he agreed to a personal visit, the other that we saw the manuscript before it was published. I don't know why I insisted on trying to meet this monster face to face. I suspect I thought it was too easy for him to hide behind a pen and paper and to make excuses. Perhaps, if we met person to person, he would let something slip which would lead us to Keith Bennett's body.

Whatever the reason, it didn't matter in the end. Brady continued to avoid a meeting. He blamed his doctors and the prison authorities, saying they wouldn't give permission. But Lord Longford never had any problems. He treated Brady's prison like a second home. It looked as if we were getting nowhere. Brady's letters were getting more and more repetitive. He blamed it on not getting the proper medication and admitted that he forgot things easily and repeated himself.

While there was a chance of getting more useful information out of him, I was prepared to steel myself to write to Brady. But it all became too much of a strain. I could only read his letters by holding them at arm's length, pinching a corner between my finger and thumb, keeping them as far away as possible.

Finally, I could write no more. Alan took over. He

wrote to Brady telling him that if he was not prepared to meet our conditions we were withdrawing our approval of his book.

On 5 January 1991, he wrote back: 'If you wish to now withdraw your support, please state so in writing. I have nothing to gain from the project except additional trouble and public abuse. I will be glad to scrap the whole thing.'

But he carried on with the book.

On 16 July 1991, he wrote: 'The book is finished, complete with diagrams, maps, lists, photographs and other documentary evidence.

'Please state to me in writing whether you, your wife and family still support the truth being published. If you do not, the book will not be published until after my death.'

He knew our attitude, but kept ignoring the fact that we had changed our minds.

And in October 1991, he issued a statement to the newspapers, referring to our initial letter of support and virtually accusing us of lying about giving our approval.

I had just spent several weeks in hospital. I'd found a lump in my breast and needed urgent surgery. It was some time before I had got enough strength back to reply to Brady's outrageous accusations. But when I had I told Alan: 'It's time the gloves came off. He's gone too far.'

On 15 October I wrote to Brady: 'Brady, How dare you slag my husband and myself regarding this so-called book of yours. You say it will keep Myra Hindley in prison forever. Well, why haven't you given this information, if there is any, to the DPP?

'You want us to do things to help you, but you cannot face me and I know for a fact that it is up to you, not the doctors. If you are clever enough to write a book, prison is the place for you, not hospital.

'I am the one who should be afraid of facing you, not the other way round. What are you afraid of? Home truths?

'You are the one who always said you believe in action not words. Well, I am the one who is about to get the action started, believe me. No more playing cat and mouse. You are nothing but a con man. Did I say man? I mean monster.

'Hindley will never get out of prison. The nation won't allow it. So we don't need your help. After all the hurt you have caused so many people, how dare you slag me!

'You will never get our permission for any book or anything that helps you. So go ahead and BURN it.'

And I warned him: 'Years ago, you were fighting a sick woman. But I am as strong as a lion and getting stronger every day. I have the Lord with me, not the devil. I don't suppose you have the guts to answer this.'

I was right. A couple of days later, his response dropped through the letterbox. As Alan opened the long, brown envelope my own letter, addressed to 490 I. Brady, Park Lane Hospital, Maghull, Liverpool, fell out.

Scribbled on the front were the words 'Do not issue.' And scrawled across the back in big, blue letters, was the message 'Do not issue. Return sender.'

Inside, was my last letter to Brady – torn into 16 little pieces.

I must admit, my reaction was a mixture of contempt and relief. I was glad it was all over.

Every word I wrote to that monster was dragged screaming from my very soul. There were times when I was physically sick writing them. No matter how often I wrote, it never got easier. Every letter was a nightmare come to life.

One of the doctors at the hospital once warned me to beware of Brady. 'He is a cunning and crafty man,' he said, 'and he is out to manipulate you.' But I was doing the same to him and I am only sad it didn't work completely. I wanted Pauline and Keith returned to their families. At least Pauline was found and I am convinced that would never have happened if I hadn't written to Brady. I still wonder if I could have actually gone through with the ordeal of meeting the man who butchered my daughter face to face.

I think I could. It would have taken every ounce of courage and determination I had left. But I would have taken a Valium, braced myself and told him: 'You know why I am here. Don't waste my time. You are going to die in here. So just tell me what I want to know and let me get on with the rest of my life.'

17

Last night Alan and I noticed the smell of freesias again. For a year or so we have noticed it intermittently. Each time there were no flowers in the house and no perfume that could be confused with that distinctive scent. Last night we smiled at each other: we both understood that Lesley was close to us again. Freesias had always been my favourite flowers and in the summer of 1964 Lesley had brought back from her holiday with the church in North Wales a small bottle of freesia perfume. Although she had not had a great deal of spending money she had bothered to bring me back that small bottle. The gesture touched me. It was typical of Lesley. The mysterious smell of freesias that is sensed in odd rooms in the house so frequently of late convinces us that Lesley is close to us once again. Of course she is in our hearts and minds every day and every night, but the scent of freesias that has lately become noticeable puts Lesley almost in my arms again.

It has been difficult for the boys, growing up in the shadow of their sister's tragic and controversial death. They have coped very well considering the pressures upon them. It is sometimes difficult to realise that the boys are now of a similar age to Alan and me at the time of Lesley's death. They have children of their own, some of whom are a similar age to Lesley at the time she was taken away from us. These grandchildren are a blessing and, although they can never replace our Lesley, are a constant reminder of the child-like innocence and trust that she represented. I have ten surviving grandchildren, all of them kind and loving in their different ways.

I suppose the over-protective attitude to the boys which Alan and I unconsciously adopted after Lesley's death must have rubbed off in their treatment of their own children. As I look back through our photograph albums I realise how wary we were about letting photographs be taken of the lads. We took our own, of course, but were adamant that no press photos be taken. In none of the numerous press features that have appeared over the years are there pictures of Terry, Tommy or Brett. This was a conscious decision on our part, based on our fear that one day Brady or Hindley might get out of prison and take another of our children in some warped kind of revenge. This may seem far-fetched, perhaps, but a gaol break is not the only way for a child-murderer to get out of gaol nowadays. The activities of confused 'do-gooders' could have the Myra Hindleys of this world stalking the streets tomorrow if anyone were ever to listen to them. Hindley knows of my deep loathing for her and I want my children and grandchildren to be safe from that pervert's evil plans.

I do accept that at times I have verged on the hysterical in my attempts to keep the boys safe. I am sure that they could all tell stories of their mum causing them embarrassment in front of their mates and girlfriends. One incident perhaps illustrates the extent to which I struggled to ensure that I knew where they were at all times.

One evening I started to get rather fidgety as Tommy had not returned home. It was mid-evening but he had not rung to explain why he hadn't returned for his supper. I should add that Tommy had turned 21 by this time! My imagination went into overdrive and I had started to convice myself that he had gone to watch a Manchester United match in Holland without informing me. I always insisted that Tommy or Brett phone me so that I knew where they were when they were not at home. Terry was older and had left home by this time. I sat and fumed and was getting myself into an agitated state. Suddenly I decided to check his usual haunts.

Although by now it was late evening I tracked him down at a pub not so far away. I saw him sitting at a table with some of his mates. I was furious. He had his back to me and didn't see me approaching. Some of his friends saw me coming and started to edge away. I think I had developed something of a reputation for my protectiveness (although I am sure they probably had another word for it). To Tommy's obvious embarrassment I gave him a strong dressing-down in front of his chums, demanding to know why he had not telephoned me. There were a few sniggers from the table and eventually, to Tommy's further humiliation, I ended up marching him out of the pub. I cringe at the thought of it now, but the effect of losing a child like Lesley makes a mother behave oddly sometimes.

I tried my best to ensure that the boys were disrupted as little as possible in their growing up and schooling. When we were forced to move because of press harassment we arranged for Terry to continue his schooling without interruption by having him stay with my good friend Margaret Glennen. He was a bit of a rover at first and took some time to recover from the feelings of guilt he nursed for not having accompanied Lesley to the fair that fatal night. He trained for butchery, travelled the world with the Merchant Navy and eventually settled down to self-employment. He has been married twice and has given us four grandchildren: Charlene Lesley, Alan, Paul and Terri Louise.

Tommy has also been married twice, but his first child, Scott, tragically suffered a cot death and is buried with Lesley at Southern Cemetery. He has three children surviving, however: Lesley Ann, Clint and a baby daughter named Claire Louise. It is a wonderful comfort to be surrounded by such boisterous and caring grandchildren. It may be a cliché to say so, but they do help to keep one young and forward-looking.

Brett, who was the baby of the family, probably suffered from my protectiveness more than his brothers. He remembers Lesley least well because of his age, but has recollections of her teaching him to ride his little red bike and it was Lesley who taught him to walk. She mothered him, and if circumstances had been different I feel they would have had a very close relationship over the years. Brett now has three girls: Melissa Ann, Donna Marie and little Brettina Leanne.

Just as Alan and I adopted a regime of close care and attention in bringing up the boys, so have they with their own children. This is probably unconscious, although they too are aware of the potential danger that exists from Hindley or other perverts who are stimulated by her example. The beasts still cast their ugly shadow down the years. In their different schools all the teachers know that our grandchildren are connected with the family that suffered, with others, all those years ago.

Since the events that ripped our lives apart, Christmas has remained a traumatic experience. As the festival approaches I look forward to the gathering of the boys and their children at our house with all the optimism and love that the season stimulates. At the same time I cannot help but feel each year the chill that cuts through the happiness. Boxing Day and all its memories and associations is a day to be endured, somehow, without upsetting the children with my inevitable tears. The grandchildren who are old enough to understand are very good about 'grandmother's quietness'. They offer innocent support and comfort, but sometimes the little mannerisms they have which remind me of Lesley bring it all back. Of course she lives for us through them, but Alan and I always make a conscious effort to ensure that we always treat them as individuals in their own right and not as substitutes for Lesley.

In the dead mid-winter of the year we sit together and take silent joy in the life that goes on, and the rebirth of hope. In different ways we all feel that Lesley is with us and we are not miserable, but the holiday can never be for us as it is for others. It is a time for memories and reflections on what might have been.

If things had been different there would be another child to join us in our celebrations of the season. The explanation of this goes back to 1971. There was a television campaign at the time urging families to foster or adopt children. At this time Alan was in a decent job and we felt that we wanted to do something for those who were worse off than ourselves. We were certainly in a unique position to know how careful one has to be in protecting children in a potentially violent society. We put in an application and received the appropriate forms.

I must admit that I wanted to adopt a girl. It was not an attempt to have a substitute for Lesley. No one could ever replace her. I had a fund of love that I wanted to give and from which a girl would have benefited best. We received two visits from a female official of the adoption agency concerned and all seemed to be going well. Alan had even prepared a bedroom in our house and we had a good home ready and waiting for some little child. We seemed to have satisfied all the requirements and were excited at the prospect of our 'new' child. Then we received our third visit.

I could tell by the coolness of the official's manner that all was not well. She came straight to the point.

'Why didn't you tell me who you are?'

What on earth was she on about? We had filled forms in till we were weary. I asked her what she was talking about. She persisted in her demands to know why we had 'hidden' the fact of having a murdered daughter. I could feel my blood boiling. She persisted in demanding to know why we hadn't mentioned this fact in the section of the form headed 'Other Remarks'. It was ridiculous. I could control myself no longer. Yet again there seemed to be no natural justice and I burst out, '*I* didn't kill Lesley! She was murdered by others, you know! Perhaps you've forgotten *those* details!'

It was as if we had hidden some guilty secret from this agent of bureaucracy. She kept repeating that we should have told her. Alan and I couldn't believe that this insensitive woman was turning us down because of something that had been done to us some years before. Everything seemed to be upside-down. We were being treated as suspects again. All we wanted to do was to give a loving home to a child without parents. And so the official left and no child ever came to share our home.

Seldom does a visit from one of the boys or the grandchildren go by without some little reference to Lesley. Only the other day some chance remark made me remember a laugh we had with Lesley over a confusion in her happy little mind. Mary Waugh had told me of a time when Lesley had come into her shop for some sweeties. She had enquired of Lesley how the family was and had been told that Brett was suffering from German measles. Lesley must have looked concerned because Mary started to reassure her that Brett would be all right. 'Oh yes,' said Lesley, 'it will be all right. Daddy speaks German, you see.' When Mary told me that later we collapsed in laughter. For a time it became something of a family joke.

We are quite a close-knit family and I have tried to ensure that what happened to Lesley has not intruded more than need be into the lives of the boys or our grandchildren, but there have been occasions when it has been very difficult to stop those who would try to make a profit out of the horror and grief caused by the child-molesters and killers Brady and Hindley. Apart from the distress that is caused to my family I have felt there were times when the sheer bad taste of certain individuals had to be curbed for the sake of decency, and to stop a 'loony' cult following, focused on Brady and Hindley, from developing.

It is difficult to believe but in the last twelve years I have had to intervene three times in order to stop the presentation of stage plays which feature Brady and Hindley as their central characters. I am pleased to say that although it was not easy to achieve I was successful in each case. I know that this is not a romantic age and that the theatrical hero is no longer necessarily a 'nice guy', but attempting to portray in the name of entertainment beasts like the two who killed my child and so many others is beyond decency.

About ten years after Brady and Hindley were locked away I received a phone call from a London newspaper informing me that a fringe theatre in Islington was about to put on a play about the Moors Murders. I made contact over the phone with the director but he failed to understand my point of view. The play went ahead. I had briefed a lawyer who went down to London to see the opening night. He was disgusted by the presentation, which even featured a tape-recording of a child screaming in agony. Whatever point the play might have been trying to make was lost in effects and sensationalism. It clearly exploited grief and terror and pandered to the lowest appetites in human nature. We threatened to sue and the play closed after its opening night.

The next attempt to present the sordid horrors of Brady and Hindley's rampage of slaughter took place closer to home, in 1983. A contact in the local Manchester press rang me to warn of a play that had been put together by some Manchester University students. It was based entirely on the reign of terror that the pair had indulged in twenty years previously. I telephoned the Dean of the university to get it stopped. I think he felt rather reluctant to be seen interfering in the students' freedom of expression so he gave me the address and phone number of the student/actor who was responsible.

If the Dean felt some reluctance to inhibit student

freedom I certainly did not. I spoke to John Royle very frankly. I think he was somewhat taken aback to be confronted by somebody who was directly affected by the events he was planning to portray on stage. To him it was just a theoretical case that offered lots of dramatic potential. To me it was a flesh-and-blood daughter who died a nightmare death. It took some time to get this point over to him. For a university student he seemed remarkably slow at realising the significance of what he planned to do.

I asked Royle if he had a sister or other relative of Lesley's age, but the implication seemed to be lost on him. He seemed determined to persevere with his scheme in order to earn dramatic credit from the grief of others. I could stand it no longer and broke down in tears. Suddenly I could hear him apologising and promising to give up his scheme. Perhaps the reality of what he was playing at finally became clear to him. I think that young man learned a lesson during that phone call which a lifetime of university lectures might fail to teach.

Finally I learned from another newspaper contact that yet another Moors Murder play was about to go into production. This was at a theatre connected with the former newsreader Richard Whitmore. I immediately contacted Mr Whitmore and asked him to explain why such an obscene drama should be presented. He claimed with great charm that he had no direct influence on the material presented as at that time he was simply letting theatre space to the people concerned. I expressed doubt that his responsibility could be so easily shrugged off, but he did give me the number of the 18-year-old actor whose brainchild the production was.

I spoke to him and he verified that the play was indeed about Brady and Hindley and their murders. He spoke with some pride of the fact that he expected to make quite a name for himself playing the part of Ian Brady. I scornfully reminded him that he wasn't even born when the events took place. He seemed immune to my appeals and I demanded to speak to his mother. She was a reasonable woman but like her son was too involved with the project to understand the damage that could result. Neither seemed to consider the implications of presenting a murderer to audiences in a potentially heroic light. I realised that most decent people would see him for what he is, but the lunatic fringe might well see something glamorous in Brady's crackpot 'philosophy' and deeds. The heartache caused to those who have lost children to murderers was lost on both mother and son. She eventually promised to 'have a word with him'.

I felt a cold rage sweep over me. I thought of Lesley and those other bodies buried on the moor. I thought of the boys and their vulnerable children. I thought of all the other children taken by sadists and casual killers year after year. This ambitious young man was not going to make his name at their expense. I told him with icy firmness that if he went ahead with his play I would pursue him through every channel of the media that would listen to me. I promised to blast him with such publicity that no theatre would ever employ him again.

He was not the type who had a better nature one could appeal to, so I battered him with threats that I had every intention of following up. He quickly backed off after I had poured scorn on his claim that he was only doing the play 'in order to inform the public'.

The play never went on.

The fight always goes on. So long as there are those who are prepared to make profit of various kinds out of private grief I shall fight to frustrate their plans. Every time I hear of some new play or book or article that is clearly designed to exploit the public's morbid desire for sensationalism I think of Lesley, John Kilbride, Edward Evans, Pauline Reade, Keith Bennett and the countless other lost souls who died bleak and lonely deaths away from their mothers and families. The fight then becomes very easy.

It is not only financial profit that some people seek to make out of their association with the victims and villains of society. People like Lord Longford have kept themselves in the public eye by constant association with dangerous deviants such as Myra Hindley, the Black Panther, Peter Sutcliffe, Dennis Nilsen, and so on. People like him will satisfy their desire to be constantly in the public eye by repeated and deliberately outrageous defences of those for whom there can be no defence. In the guise of Christians or humanitarians they choose to be blind to the need for justice. Driven by an egotistical mania they proclaim their claptrap on television and radio, adopting stances that might make them a mockery in all right-minded people's eyes but which feed their craving for a sickly limelight. These types are as obnoxious and dangerous as those with whom they so freely associate – the poisonous dregs of humanity.

I thank God that there is still some beauty in the world. There are the little children who have yet to learn how hard the world can be. There are the innocent smiles on the faces of my grandchildren. There is sometimes the mysterious smell of freesias to remind me of the tenderest beauty I ever knew in this world. And there is Melissa Ann, my grandchild, with her uncanny resemblance to the daughter I lost.

18

And so life goes on. Looking back at the past for the purposes of this book, trying to get the agonising events of my life into order and the terrible details accurately recorded, has been a painful experience. Yet it soon became apparent to me that, despite the struggles with grief and drugs and certain ruthless individuals, there has been a positive streak running through it all. Sometimes this has led to behaviour and events that I might wish had turned out differently in detail, but always I have been driven by a deep desire to ensure that in matters relating to Lesley in particular, and child murder in general, right should prevail.

It was to this end that I established the Murder Victims' Association, in February 1985. The MVA has been involved with petitions to the government concerning issues of imprisonment and parole as well as holding regular meetings in which we try to help relatives of victims to deal with their terrible sorrow. The hard-won energy I have always put into my personal campaign to ensure that Brady and Hindley remain behind bars has been channelled into a cause that aims to help other parents to cope with the unique agony of losing a child or loved one to a murderer. Our group offers a shoulder to cry on, advice based on bitter experience about coping with deep misery, and practical help in dealing with the bureaucracy of murder, including claims to the Criminal Injuries Compensation Board, dealing with the media, etc. Our monthly meetings have genuinely helped a distressingly large number of victims with therapeutic assistance at a traumatic time in their lives. We know that grief lasts a lifetime, but at times of crisis, whenever they occur, we are ready to offer help. I wish such an organisation had existed when Lesley was taken from me. If it had, then maybe my life would not have contained so many lost years.

It will have been obvious from what I have written that I have a deep loathing for Ian Brady and Myra Hindley. To feel otherwise would be unnatural – as unnatural as the treatment they made my Lesley suffer. I cannot claim to have reached the point of forgiveness, even after a quarter of a century; indeed, maybe my feelings are even stronger as I look back and review the 25 broken years for which they are responsible. I have tried to be a decent Christian and have retained my faith in God throughout this time, but I know that there are certain aspects of belief and ability to worship in which I am lacking. I cannot help this, but I cannot expect people who have not been in a similar situation to myself to understand it. My 'deficient' Christianity is best illustrated, perhaps, by describing my version of the Lord's Prayer: I cannot bring myself to speak the words, 'Forgive us our trespasses as we forgive those who trespass against us.'

To a fundamentalist Christian this may seem a terrible admission, but it is the truth. I would be a hypocrite if I said those words because they would *not* be the truth. I cannot forgive Ian Brady and Myra Hindley. I do not think I ever will. I thought I was unique in my restricted form of Christianity until quite recently when I began talking to a lady named Ann Robinson after we had both taken part in a television programme. Ann, too, was the mother of a murdered child and we discussed how our lives had been affected in all sorts of small ways as well as major ones. It was with a spasm of relief that I heard her admitting in a rather shame-faced way that she could not bring herself to say those same words in the Lord's Prayer. What a tragically isolated group we are . . . the unconsidered victims of a murderer's casual act of horror.

It will have become clear that I am not in good health. Like many other surviving parents, I too am a victim of my child's murderers. But I do survive. I will go on. Some say it is hate that keeps me alive and in some ways that is true. I have said it myself on occasions. It is not quite as simple as it may sound. I do have hate. I also have a profound love that keeps me going. My love is for Alan, who has been at my side through so much, for Terry and Tommy and Brett with their patient good humour in such difficult circumstances, for my grandchildren, who bring joy and optimism into my life. There are so many to love and go on living for; and there is Lesley . . . always Lesley.

It is the love I bear for Lesley and those from whom she was separated that causes the hatred I nurse for those who cold-bloodedly took her away. It is hatred *and* love that keep me going. I will cling to life with every fibre of will that survives in my body so that I can ensure justice is done and the life sentences that Brady and Hindley are serving continue for the rest of their lives.

Outside my window the leaves are still clinging to the trees. It is getting colder. Soon it will be time to think of Christmas and presents for the grandchildren. It will be time to prepare for that special visit to Lesley's grave. Although I go every week to tidy the little plot and leave fresh flowers for my daughter the visit at Christmas is very important. This Christmas it will be extra special as it will be a quarter of a century since Lesley skipped off happily to the fair and untimely death. It seems only yesterday that she gave us a little hug and went off with her sixpence to seek a little fun and entertainment before returning for her tea with all of us. We know she will never come back, but still we wait. Soon we will be reunited. Soon we will be at peace, with each other again.

So many wasted years . . . so many tears . . . so many thoughts of what might have been. It is very quiet at the cemetery on Boxing Day. We are usually on our own as we visit our little girl. It is not a depressing place – far from it. From where we stand this Christmas we will be able to hear the hum of traffic and life going on beyond the peaceful setting for Lesley's last resting-place. It is good that this should be so. Lesley loved life with all the enthusiasm and spirit of the young. We will stand and say a little prayer for the child who was so innocent of the ways of the world. Maybe some last shrivelled leaves will still be clinging to the ash trees and oaks that line the boundaries of the cemetery. I hope the sky is clear. From where Lesley lies the foul hump of Saddleworth Moor is hidden. She rests at last. There is calm in her soft blue eyes, I know. I like to think of her gazing at the branches of the oak and the ash and the clear blue sky that promises so much at the year's turning. Sleep on, my dearest Lesley. Nobody can hurt you now. You are safe at last. The world has done its worst. We will be with each other soon, I promise you.

Tonight, as always, I will talk to you. You will be patient as usual and indulge an old woman's needs. Since losing you in this life I have hoped that you can hear me as I tell you all the things there was never time to say. There will be time eventually . . . all the time in the world.

Dearest Lesley, I wish there had been more time. We took it for granted that there were all the years and the seasons left for us to love each other in. There was so little time, wasn't there? So many things left unsaid . . . so many things left undone.

Do you remember the bridal shop in Oldham Road that you always insisted on stopping at when we were in town? There was a particular dress that you would look at longingly every time we went past. I recall you saying, 'Mummy, when I'm old enough and get married I want a dress like that.' Yet you were not allowed to grow any older. You would have been a good mother, I know.

There have been so many places that I wish you could have visited with us. We never go on a holiday or visit anywhere new without Alan or me saying 'Lesley would have liked this,' or 'I wish Lesley were here to enjoy this with us.' But then we usually feel your presence and know that you are there with us in spirit.

Your brothers miss you, Lesley. They have children now, some as old as you were then. I wish that you could have had children of your own. They would have been such beautiful boys and girls if they had taken after you. At least you have some fine nephews and nieces. They often ask about their 'Aunty Lesley' when they come to the house and look at your photogrpahs. You would have got on so well with them, my darling.

There is so much to say, Lesley. Every day I think of you and remember so many happy times together. I try to forget the bad things that happened to you. I miss you, Lesley. We all do. Be at peace . . . be happy . . . I will talk to you again . . . very soon.

I love you, Lesley.

Postscript

I never cease to wonder how this frail body of mine keeps on going. You would think the angina, heart operation, Valium addiction and the operation to remove the cancer from my ovaries would have been enough to drain the last dregs of strength from someone much stronger than me. But no matter what fate throws at me, I somehow survive.

Is it luck – or something more?

By May of 1991, I was taking 18 pills a day for my various ailments ranging from asthma to angina. I was permanently short of breath but sitll smoking 40 cigarettes a day. My doctor didn't like it, but he told me stress was more of a potential killer than cigarettes and he would rather see me smoking than breaking down in tears from the pressure of life.

But one night, I had real difficulty breathing. Alan rang the doctor. He said it could be a couple of hours before an ambulance arrived. Alan wasn't prepared to wait. He bundled me into the car and drove me to Withington Hospital.

It turned out I had pneumonia and the doctors said if he had waited for the ambulance, I wouldn't have survived the night.

I was released after five days, but within two weeks, I was back again. This time, I had found lumps in my breast and was scared. I'd been watching a TV programme about breast cancer which said women should check themselves regularly. I began to probe just out of interest and found a lump. Alan confirmed there was something there and a few weeks later I had two cancerous tumours removed from my breast. Even the thought of cancer sends shivers of terror through most people. Not me. Surprisingly, when the doctor told me I had cancer, I stayed remarkably calm. I worried about what might happen to Alan if I didn't pull through. I didn't want to leave him. But if I didn't survive, I would be able to see my Lesley again. I was in a unique position. Because I wanted to be with my Lesley, I didn't have the fears any normal woman might have. I had waited over 25 years to see my little girl again and if I was destined to go, I didn't mind at all. I suspect I was even looking forward to leaving behind all the pain and the heartache and the tears, to holding Lesley in my arms again and spending eternity with her. But it was not to be. Two weeks after the operation, I was given the all clear and returned home to await the next, almost inevitable, blow which fate seemed determined to throw at me.

It came on Lesley's birthday, 21 August 1992. She would have been 37.

Her grave always looks a treat. But at Christmas and on her birthday, we make a special effort. Alan and I spent two hours clearing the dead flowers, filling the pots and covering the grave with masses of white roses and tiger lilies. I use as many white flowers as I can because they are pure. We wrapped her birthday cards in clingfilm to keep the weather out and placed them carefully among the flowers. When we had finished, it looked a real picture.

We'd only been home an hour when the phone rang. It was my daughter-in-law, Marion, and she insisted on talking to Alan. He listened for a minute, put the phone down, turned to me and said: 'Somebody's desecrated Lesley's grave'.

I felt sick. I couldn't believe my ears. Surely nobody could be so sick.

Alan insisted I stayed at home while he went to see what had happened. The flower pots had been knocked over and thrown aside, the flowers scattered all over the grass and a little rose bush we had planted uprooted and trampled on. The birthday cards with our messages of love had vanished. And scratched all over the pure, white marble were the sickening messages – 'Let Myra free', 'Let Myra go'.

Whoever it was had scratched the monster's name

above Lesley's, all over the back of the stone and even along the base. They'd used a ball-point pen and, when it ran out, they'd carried on using it like a nail. It needs a special kind of perverted mind to do something like that and I am convinced it was some of Hindley's followers. What sickens me is that they must have been in hiding, watching us prepare Lesley's grave all the time.

Only a few yards from Lesley's is the grave of Edward Evans, the 17-year-old boy who was Hindley and Brady's last victim. Whenever we have flowers left over, I always put them on Edward's grave. I'd made a nice little display that day. But when we got back to the cemetery, that too had been destroyed. The pot was torn up and the flowers thrown aside. It had to be someone who had been watching me all the time. No one else would have known about Edward's grave. And no one but Hindley's followers could have been so sick in the head as to desecrate two innocent people's graves.

I wrote to Hindley: 'I hope you are satisfied with what your evil followers have done to my child's grave. Can you not let her rest in peace? You can't hurt Lesley any more, so now you are starting on me.

'I know the cards were taken for a reason – to prove to you that the dirty deed had been done. If you are what you say you are – a good Christian, Catholic girl – be truthful and tell me whether you had anything to do with this sickening act because I am always going to blame you for it.'

I expected her to reply denying it since she is supposed to be a reformed character. But there was only silence. And that, to me, speaks volumes.

The whole sorry episode left me devastated again. I spent days wondering if there is going to be no end to all this. What can possibly go wrong next?

Two weeks later, I was back in hospital. Another operation. The cancer was back, this time in my bowels, and three tumours were removed.

I'm still having treatment, still weak, still one half of me telling me it would be easier to give up and go to Lesley, the other half insisting I should stay and keep up the fight to make sure Hindley spends the rest of her days behind bars. She is due for another parole hearing in 1995 and has been boasting to friends that this time she will be freed.

I've decided to stick around. I've got a lot to say about that.

Warner now offers an exciting range of quality titles by both established and new authors. All of the books in this series are available from:
Little, Brown and Company (UK) Limited,
Cash Sales Department,
P.O. Box 11,
Falmouth,
Cornwall TR10 9EN.

Alternatively you may fax your order to the above address. Fax No. 0326 376423.

Payments can be made as follows: Cheque, postal order (payable to Little, Brown and Company) or by credit cards, Visa/Access. Do not send cash or currency. UK customers: and B.F.P.O.: please send a cheque or postal order (no currency) and allow £1.00 for postage and packing for the first book, plus 50p for the second book, plus 30p for each additional book up to a maximum charge of £3.00 (7 books plus).

Overseas customers including Ireland, please allow £2.00 for postage and packing for the first book, plus £1.00 for the second book, plus 50p for each additional book.

NAME (Block Letters) ....

ADDRESS..

....

☐ I enclose my remittance for _____

☐ I wish to pay by Access/Visa Card

Number [ ][ ][ ][ ][ ][ ][ ][ ][ ][ ][ ][ ][ ][ ][ ][ ]

Card Expiry Date [ ][ ][ ][ ]